PEACE IN THE MIDDLE EAST:
THE CHALLENGE FOR ISRAEL

Peace in the Middle East:
The Challenge for Israel

edited by
EFRAIM KARSH

FRANK CASS

First published in 1994 in Great Britain by
FRANK CASS & CO. LTD.
900 Eastern Avenue, Newbury Park
Ilford, Essex IG2 7HH, England

and in the United States of America by
FRANK CASS
c/o International Specialized Book Services, Inc.
5804 N.E. Hassalo Street
Portland, Oregon 97213-3644

British Library Cataloguing in Publication Data

Peace in the Middle East: Challenge for
Israel
I. Karsh, Efraim
327.1720956

ISBN 0-7146-4614-8 (hardback)
0-7146-4141-3 (paperback)

Library of Congress Cataloging in Publication Data

A catalog record of this book is available from the
Library of Congress

This group of studies first appeared in a Special
Issue on 'Peace in the Middle East: The Challenge
for Israel' of *Israel Affairs*, Vol.1, No.1, Autumn
1994, published by Frank Cass & Co. Ltd.

Typeset by Vitaset, Paddock Wood, Kent
Printed in Great Britain by
Watkiss Studios Ltd, Biggleswade, Beds

Contents

Introduction

EFRAIM KARSH

AS IT approaches its fiftieth anniversary, the State of Israel seems closer than ever to its professed loftiest ideal: contractual peace with all its Arab neighbours, first and foremost the Palestinians. The Declaration of Principles on Palestinian Interim Self-Government Arrangements, signed on the White House Lawn on 13 September 1993, was a watershed in the one-hundred-year war between Arabs and Jews. After a century of denial and rejection, of blood-letting and bereavement, Arabs and Jews have finally agreed to bury the hatchet and settle for peace, based on mutual recognition and acceptance. Jordan followed the Palestinian example within a day by signing a joint agenda with Israel on the framework for peace. Even President Hafiz Asad of Syria, the paragon of Arab rejection of the fact of Israel, has been grudgingly reconciling himself to the idea of a fully-fledged peace with the Jewish state.

This is neither to ignore the problems and obstacles that lie ahead, nor to discount the disruptive power of extremists on both sides, as starkly demonstrated by the Hebron, Afula and Hadera massacres. Yet, even the most implacable foes of the Israeli–Palestinian agreement would concede that it has changed the Middle Eastern political landscape beyond recognition. The Rabin–Arafat handshake; the countless working sessions between Israel and the PLO; the bursts of joy in Gaza and Jericho on the arrival of the first Palestinian policemen; visits by Israeli officials to Gulf emirates and their hosts' open endorsement for close economic relations with Israel, all these images of the rapidly changing Middle East are unlikely to evaporate into thin air in the face of future setbacks, which are bound to accompany the historic reconciliation between Arabs and Jews.

This volume explores the significance and implications of the nascent peace process for Israel, its security, economic well-being and international standing. In the opening contribution, P.J. Vatikiotis, a long-time observer of Middle Eastern affairs, casts a personal gloss on the Arab–Israeli peace process. He views the Israeli–Palestinian accord as "the best news I have had in fifty years of living with this conflict", and believes that the mutual resignation to the notion of peaceful coexistence, embedded in the agreement, can readily culminate in comprehensive peace and regional cooperation. However, were Arabs and Israelis to prove unable to surmount the acrimonious legacy between them – and Vatikiotis considers religious–cultural rejectionism as peace's worst enemy – then a physical separation between these two communities or nations must be effected, with international forces interposed between them as a buffer.

This cautious optimism is shared by other writers. According to Dov Zakheim, while peace will allow Israel to rationalize its defence expenditures and restructure its armed forces, it will still need to maintain a strong military posture "to account not only for threats from states not willing to subscribe to a settlement at all, but those that might renege on it". This, in turn, will demand considerable resources that will probably "wipe out any chance of peace dividend, other than that which might be realized through increased military sales abroad". That, however, "remains a small price to pay for obtaining what Israel has sought since its birth: a reduced threat of war and therefore, a far less stressful existence for its citizens".

A more sanguine assessment of the economic implications of peace is offered by Ben-Zion Zilberfarb. Although sceptical of peace's direct economic gains, such as a trade boom between Israel and the Palestinian autonomy, or for that matter between Israel and the wider Arab world, he deems the indirect effects of peace to be highly beneficial to the Israeli economy. These include trade relations with countries which hitherto refused to trade with Israel, and a possible increase in foreign direct investments. Above all, he estimates that a gradual reduction in military outlays and its diversion to development investments may increase Israel's economic output by $35 billion over a ten-year period, a substantial gain indeed.

Where Israel has already reaped a substantial "peace dividend" is in the critical realm of "Israel among the nations". The "special relation-ship" with the United States, which plunged to one of its lowest ebbs during the latter part of the Bush presidency, has made an impressive recovery following Labour's ascendency in June 1992 and the resultant reinvigoration of the peace process; so have Israel's relations with the European Community. Yet while Bernard Reich expects the US–Israeli relationship to retain its uniqueness for the foreseeable future, if not without occasional frictions and disagreements, Rosemary Hollis is more sceptical on how close Israel's relations with the European Union can become. Not only have the West Europeans been more lukewarm than their American counterparts towards Israel over the past decades; not only do the internal politics of the European Union and the fear of economic competition preclude a full Israeli member-ship, but "from the perspective of the EU, Israel is and will remain part of the Middle East".

The peace dividend, argues Aharon Klieman, has not been confined to Israel's enhanced standing and active re-engagement with the international community; it has also mitigated the wariness and distrust with which Israelis tend to view the outside world, ushering in a greater spirit of openness and self-assurance. In the words of Prime Minister Yitzhak Rabin: "We have got to rescue ourselves from the pervading sense of isolation gripping us for the better part of a half-century. We must join the worldwide movement towards peace, conciliation and cooperation, for otherwise we shall be left behind, standing alone at the station platform." One special relationship that has already been affected by this buoyant mood, and is certain to undergo a fundamental transformation as the peace process unfolds, is that between Israel and the Jewish diaspora. As Max Beloff puts it,

> One has the impression that Israel's ambassadors increasingly see their relations with the local Jewish community as one of expounding the Israeli government's own position and less than it used to be of seeking the opinions of their interlocutors . . . As the demographic changes make their effect, indifference to what the diaspora can do is likely to grow. What matters will be what happens in Israel and the rest will be marginal. If some form of peace ensures security, even the American Jewish lobby will cease to be valued.

Before peace can ensure security, however, some hurdles have yet to be crossed. Tall among these stand the Israeli settlements in the occupied territories, the West Bank in particular, which have arguably made the surrender of these lands to Arab control inconceivable. Not so, maintains Elisha Efrat. If anything, the fact that only 120,000 Jews, a mere three per cent of Israel's Jewish population, have made the West Bank their home, speaks volumes of the lack of public support for this endeavour. This, together with the small size of many of these settlements and their wide geographical distribution, means that most of them will wither away as peace strikes root.

No less daunting a task confronting Arabs and Israelis will be the demarcation of their future borders, for no other reason than that it impinges on such existential issues as retention of strategic depth and control over water resources and arable lands. To prevent a deadlock, Moshe Brawer advises peacemakers on both sides to avoid rigid adherence to past boundaries. There is nothing sacred in either the colonial borders or the lines established in the wake of the 1948–49 War, he argues, as both were dictated by practical considerations of the time, which were largely mindless of the needs of the local inhabitants, and have anyway been rendered obsolete by the demographic, technological, and physical changes that have taken place ever since.

Instead, the mutually agreed future boundaries should be demarcated in such a way as to enhance free contacts and cooperation, thus becoming an asset, rather than a liability, to lasting peace in the region.

One person who would whole-heartedly endorse such a recommendation is Israel's Foreign Minister, Shimon Peres. Driven by the conviction that economic self-interest should eventually impel all parties in the Middle East towards some kind of reasonable accommodation, and that deep-seated grievances could be ironed out in a dialogue between rational profit-maximizers, this enlightened techno-crat has been instrumental in the attainment of the historic Israeli–Palestinian breakthrough, and is likely to play a key role in bringing it to fruition. While this vision may seem incredible to some who have had to live with and suffer from the passions generated in Middle Eastern political struggles for decades, Michael Keren shows that it has been mirrored in the views expressed by Peres's chief interlocutors, PLO officials Abu Ala and Mahmoud Abbas.

Whether and to what extent this technocratic vision is amenable to the Israeli and Palestinian communities remains to be seen. What is already clear is that the future of the peace process and all it implies will be greatly affected by the speed and degree of the economic benefits experienced by the Palestinians. For, in the final analysis, "unless those most immediately affected sense a genuine transformation in their lives commensurate with their expectations . . . similarly unrelenting pressures may work to destroy the accord. In this lies the challenge of the future."

Peace by the End of the Century?
A Personal Gloss on the
Arab–Israeli Peace Process

P.J. VATIKIOTIS

I N AUGUST 1993 the world was taken by surprise when a secretly negotiated agreement for peace between the PLO and the State of Israel was announced. What was dramatic about it was the fact that it had been negotiated secretly in Norway while the more formal and highly publicized negotiations between Israel and its Arab adversaries including the Palestinians had moved apace from the initial Madrid conference to a variety of venues, chief among them the one in Washington DC, and all of them under the auspices and good offices of the United States. Progress in these highly publicized negotiations was fitful and erratic, and a settlement of the conflict was as remote as ever, and still only a pious hope. What seemed to ensure the survival of the talks was the benevolent invigilation of a superpower, namely the United States, now under a new but as yet unsettled and untested Democrat administration in the White House. The old familiar face of the ubiquitous, smooth and aristocratic-looking Texan Secretary of States James Baker ("the deal-maker") had been succeeded by the bland, self-effacing Warren Christopher, already well known from the earlier Democrat administration of President Jimmy Carter as not the most inspiring legal or diplomatic gift to the resolution of international conflicts, and who by all accounts does not enjoy a close working relationship with President Clinton.

When asked by an Israeli friend and colleague from the University of Haifa for my reaction to the news from Norway, I replied at once: "the best news I have had in fifty years of living with this conflict". When a Palestinian acquaintance solicited my reaction, I reminded him that in the past I had often suggested that Israel was probably the only contestant in that miserable conflict who one day would have something to offer the Palestinians. One was of course aware of the difference between a Declaration of Principles and the negotiation of a

---

P.J. Vatikiotis is Emeritus Professor of Middle Eastern Politics at the University of London.

peace agreement between the PLO and Israel, entailing the ending of Israel's military occupation of the West Bank and Gaza and leading to the creation of an autonomous or independent Palestinian authority and entity in those territories. But one appreciated none the less the momentous historical and psychological significance of the secret agreement, especially as it reflected the conclusion by the protagonists that an agreement between them was essential, especially one that entailed mutual recognition, and the realization that in whatever negotiated political settlement, they will have to coexist peacefully and if necessary cooperate economically in the wider development of their region.

Clearly, the *intifada* on the West Bank and Gaza Strip could not force the ending of the Israeli occupation, nor could the Israel security forces suppress the *intifada* completely short of the use of massive and devastating military force. Compromise was inevitable in the form of a negotiated agreement. But a negotiated agreement on what premises? The Likud government rejected out of hand the formula of land for peace, the total withdrawal from the West Bank or the dismantling of Jewish settlements there, not to mention its maximalist intransigent position over Jerusalem and related matters. The PLO and a majority of Palestinians still hoped for an accommodation, including the creation of an independent Palestinian state on the West Bank to be secured for them by an outside power that could coerce Israel into agreement, namely the United States. Neither of these perceptions was realistic for it faded in the face of relentless events.

A combination of new circumstances, prominent among them the aftermath of the 1991 Gulf War (the Anglo-American Desert Storm military campaign against Saddam Hussein of Iraq for his invasion of Kuwait and the clear threat to Saudi Arabia and Western oil interests in the area, as well as to the security of Israel), the deteriorating national economy, the pressure of a new influx of Russian Jewish refugees, the heightened ideological hostility of Iran and its use of Hizballah in neighbouring Lebanon as a surrogate but real threat to Israel's security was making the Israeli electorate rather impatient with Likud's stale rejectionist and intransigent policy. Labour's allusions to a more flexible approach to a negotiated settlement with the Palestinians at least gathered momentum and attracted rather favourable publicity. Gradually the Israeli public was being introduced to the notion that all uncompromising declarations in the past to the contrary not-withstanding, the time was fast approaching when they would have to countenance direct talks with the PLO, and specifically its leader Yasir Arafat, for the resolution of the outstanding conflict between them, as well as with all their neighbouring Arab state adversaries; and that embarking upon such uncharted routes to peace would entail the making of concessions and compromises unthought of before but now considered absolutely essential to the attainment of peace; yet they hoped and insisted that these would not jeopardize the country's security. The risks were indeed great and as yet unknown, but the rewards of success even greater. The inevitability of a negotiated peace settlement between at least the Palestinians – in this case, the PLO – and Israel was already in the air after the PLO Tunis declarations in November 1988. Scattered but frequent statements by PLO-affiliated West Bank leaders and members of Arafat's political office in Tunis and elsewhere pointed unmistakably in that direction. Thus in an exchange between Faisal Husseini and Hanna Siniora[1] on one side, and the late US Ambassador Philip Habib and myself on the other at an international conference on peace in the Middle East in Lausanne in March 1989, the two West Bank Palestinian leaders conceded that there could be no direct move from occupation to autonomy without an interim or transition period. In the aftermath of the Gulf War a sense of urgency pervaded this atmosphere; everybody now emphasized the "window of opportunity" for peace in the Middle East and elsewhere. Regional conflicts were soon viewed as anachronistic blights on the emerging political conditions of the New World Order, however that was to evolve after the end of the cold war and under the auspices of the US, the only remaining superpower in the world. International euphoria in this connection ignored the unpredictable thicket that international affairs are, until it received its first shock at the hands of resurgent ethnic nationalist conflict in the Balkans and elsewhere; this in a sense made the resolution of the Palestinian–Israel conflict even more urgent; and the growing threat from the intolerant religious fundamentalists on the West Bank and Gaza, in the Jewish settlements, in neighbouring Egypt, Lebanon and Jordan and more ominously in Iran and the Sudan further afield rendered such resolution of the conflict imperative. The position and credibility of the PLO itself had been eroded and undermined by the Gulf War, when its backing of Saddam Hussein in that conflict lost it the support of oil-rich Gulf States and Saudi Arabia. Its very ability to sustain its world-wide activities and opposition to Israel was now in serious doubt.

So long as the primary responsibility for peacemaking rested mainly on the shoulders of powers external to the region of the Middle East this urgency and imperative would not be as acutely felt; and in this conflict historically the Palestinians and their Arab state allies tended to shunt or shift such responsibility to outsiders with great alacrity. Eventually it became clear that outsiders could only cobble or broker agreements which lacked the prospect of longevity, and that a way had to be found to shift back the responsibility of peacemaking to the local/ regional protagonists in the hope that these would reach agreement and then seek the assistance of outside powers for its implementation and survival.

There was some gain between the Madrid Conference and the announcement of the Oslo Agreement: Israelis, Palestinians and other Arabs (Syrians, Lebanese, Jordanians) were getting used to face-to-face negotiations over concrete issues of contention in Washington and elsewhere; recognizing all the time that peaceful accommodation or agreement between them was the only possible outcome sooner or later, in other words, inevitable.

Throughout the winter and spring of 1992 Israelis at least were anxiously considering the possibilities and ramifications of the peace process, especially in the pre-election period. Debate was intense and political alignments both shifting and unpredictable. One thing was becoming clearer as polling day in June approached: a Labour government under Rabin would risk or venture an opening towards accommodation with the Palestinians as a way of resolving the issue of the occupied territories. All this required shifts in prevailing perceptions and the use of different intellectual concepts about the peace process. Dealing with the *resolution* of a historical clash between two national communities over the possession/control of the same territory, one could no longer think in terms of a *solution* since that would entail the destruction of one or the other community, or both. More difficult was the matter of creating and introducing new sovereignty in the contested territory without destroying or rendering ineffective already existing sovereignty.

After all, the difference between the Camp David Accord of 1978 and the Oslo Agreement of 1993 is very significant: Palestinians are finally being offered if not directly and immediately, at least implicitly and eventually, something beyond a people's autonomy, namely, territorial recognition implying territorial autonomy. What is initially on offer, Gaza and Jericho, may not represent very much, but it is something and something is better than nothing. Granted that the question of Palestinian refugees and Jewish settlers on the West Bank is a difficult one, it is nevertheless negotiable. Furthermore, Jerusalem is particularly difficult, but not beyond the realm of imaginative compromise.

One way of creating or allowing new sovereignty to emerge in such a way as to be less threatening and therefore more readily acceptable to an erstwhile adversary is to place it in a larger political structure such as a "Common Market", a Middle Eastern Community (comprising at the outset Israel, Egypt and Jordan). A new sovereign political entity, a Palestinian State on the West Bank and Gaza, would emerge that is independent not behind sealed borders but in a community affording open human access and active economic and other cooperation with its neighbours across open state frontiers. The venue, or structure of a common market community assuages two emotive and mutually opposed concepts, namely, those of Palestinian sovereignty on the West Bank and Gaza and the acceptance of the territory-for-peace formula by Israel. Under a Common Market Community structure the Palestinians get their sovereign state on the West Bank and Gaza as a member of the Middle Eastern Common Market Community, recognized by all the other members of that Community, while Israel relinquishes the occupied territories within a Community arrangement in a viable dynamic new relationship with those territories and at peace with the new sovereign political authority – the Palestinian State – they will constitute.

There were many who in the closing days of the mandate in Palestine believed (out of despair?) that any scheme that required a degree of cooperation between Palestinians and Israelis was doomed. The current search is for both: cooperation, but of the kind leading to a formal and real peace between the two peoples, constituted as two separate, independent different political communities. What direct negotiations between Israeli and Palestinian representatives (since September or December 1993) have shown is that they can overcome the absolutist postures of the past in an effort to generate a climate of trust between them by risking a new kind of relationship and creating new institutions for it, despite the fact that detailed matters of border security, jurisdiction, and so on, are bitterly fought over by both sides and cause frequent hiccups and delays of several weeks or months in negotiating a final agreement between the parties; surely not an unacceptable delay in a conflict that has lasted for nearly a century. The Palestinians aim to extract as broad and generous an advantage from the Oslo Accord as the Israelis aim to keep its implementation on the ground as limited and controllable as possible. Both sides seek maximum advantage under the best possible security, the eternal quest of all political strife everywhere today as well as in the past.

What threatens the peace negotiations is the disparity between the two parties. There is an imbalance (what strategists call an asymmetry) in the political, social, economic and military strength of the two parties. The PLO, in fact the whole Palestinian and wider Arab side, appear at their weakest; its constituent parts remain highly divided, their efforts dispersed and their effectiveness dissipated. Some even believe that the lack of administrative, organizational and other related experience in the creation of new institutional and other structures among the Palestinians constitutes a serious hindrance to the negotiation of a peace agreement itself. Such weakness, however, is not of the essence, for it is only transient. A more lasting obstacle to a peace settlement is the mutual religious/cultural rejection between some of the Palestinians and their Arab allies and the Israelis. Both sides are under pressure from their respective religious fundamentalists not to reach a peaceful accommodation. Fundamentalists tend to link sanctity with power, so as to use violence in the name of God. When one believes that God promised him a particular part of the world one is inevitably exclusivist about it in a lunatic way. When politics becomes religion, the outcome is lethal, because it can only be violent. This is the problem essentially with the Jewish settler zealots on the West Bank: from the simple premise that God told them to settle there, they seem to demand that the area they occupy should be cleared of all · non-Jews.[2] Fifty years ago, Adolf Hitler was determined to dominate and control a European Continent that was free of Jews . . .! Muslim fundamentalists on the Palestinian and Arab side of the conflict believe equally that the contested territory of what was Palestine is an integral part of an exclusivist Abode or Dominion of Islam, and so sanctioned by Allah. Only Muslims must control and govern it; Israel is a usurper and an infidel interloper or intruder that must be destroyed by force if necessary and expunged from the Dominion of Islam, namely, from the Middle East.

Clearly, then, the Oslo Accord and what it is meant to achieve is opposed by elements on both sides of the conflict. Not only religious zealots but also right-wing Zionists who hold a maximalist view of what constitutes the State of Israel oppose the accord, for they will not compromise on the territorial composition of the Israeli State; they reject the formula "territory for peace". For their part, Muslim fundamentalist Palestinians will not countenance a state of Israel in any shape, size or form and therefore reject any compromise with what is there today. Furthermore, they consider any Palestinian who is prepared to compromise in this matter a traitor to the Palestinian cause and an apostate from Islam. What is interesting and may have escaped the attention of many observers is the fact that some of the more virulent and vociferous opponents of the Oslo Accord are an interesting identifiable group of Palestinian political exiles (as distinguished from refugees), most prominent among them being Dr Anis Sayegh, for long of the PLO establishment in Beirut and the Gulf, and Dr Edward Said of Columbia University, a late-comer to both Palestine and the PLO. Both are Christian and converts to the Evangelical Protestant Church. More significant is their property-owning bourgeois background in Palestine. Their families suffered great material losses when they left Palestine, and any prospect of a peace agreement with Israel is considered alongside their much higher expectations in any new Palestinian state on the West Bank. Given the likely size and nature of such a state their expectations are unrealistic. Along with numerous others, they are also the severe critics of PLO

Chairman Yasir Arafat. They oppose him because, they argue generally, he is autocratic. The difficulty is that virtually all rule and ruling institutions in the Arab Middle East have been autocratic in the main, and it is most unlikely that were any of Arafat's opponents to replace him in power, or as leaders of the PLO, they would hasten to abandon that kind of rule. To this extent one cannot take such critics too seriously, and especially when their credibility is otherwise in question.

But the problem is not only on one side of the conflict equation; the Israelis, as Jews, also suffer certain religious–cultural disabilities or obstacles they must overcome before they can consider peace-making and coexistence with an erstwhile enemy like the Palestinians and the Arab states as a matter for negotiation and compromise. Peace between the Palestinians and Israel must be a public endeavour, and there can be no endeavour in the public domain without trust, and what is lacking here between the protagonists or adversaries is trust, and ways to promote it between them. Jews have, mostly for very good reasons (mainly persecution, anti-semitism – basically a Christian invention – and related trials and tribulations mainly West of the Middle East in Christian Europe) tended to live in exclusivist and wary Jewish communities, dealing with the Gentile world around them but never quite trusting it. They seemed to cherish the notion of exile in the world. One hoped that finally the prospect of peace would help Israelis and through them Jews generally to begin to abandon their eternal mistrust and its attendant peculiarities. Similarly peace would convince Palestinians and their Arab state allies that religious–cultural rejection does not eliminate a strong and dynamic political community, or make it disappear. Having said this, one must immediately concede that consensus and compromise in the Middle East are alien political concepts, practices and conventions. They are also at a high premium, and one hoped that the Oslo Accord would introduce them in a decisive manner. One also hoped that an Israeli–Palestinian constellation in terms of combined skills, talent and joint entrepreneurship would prove a great boon to the Middle Eastern region as an irresistible force for regional development, peace and prosperity in the twenty-first century.

If, in the final analysis, Palestinians and Arabs on one side and Israelis on the other cannot or are unwilling to bridge the traditional–cultural gulf between them, because they refuse to coexist in the same corner of the world, and because their differences are irreconcilable and therefore not negotiable, one must conclude that the two communities or nations must be separated from one another. And this may require the interposition of foreign, international forces between them to keep them from clashing and in order to avoid an all-out religious war between them.[3]

NOTES

1. A leading Palestinian journalist on the West Bank.
2. As soon as I finished writing this essay, a medical doctor from the Jewish settlement of Kiryat Arba outside Hebron by the name of Baruch Goldstein, an immigrant from New York, a fanatical member of Kach and a follower of the late racist Rabbi Meir Kahane (also from New York), perpetrated the terrible massacre of Muslim Palestinians praying in the main mosque at Hebron, in the early morning of Friday 25 February 1994. Clearly a terrorist zealot with a blind hatred of Palestinians and determined to cleanse *Eretz Israel* from them, Goldstein's case highlights the deadly consequences of linking nationalism to religion, or sanctifying nationalism by a holy scripture. The lethal mix of religion and politics which seems to pervade both the Israeli and Arab sides in this conflict continues to frustrate all efforts so far at peacemaking. Mutual religious–cultural rejection by the protagonists is a mighty obstacle to reconciliation and peace between them. Nor do outsiders help. As if passions were not inflamed enough on the weekend of 25–28 February 1994 in that unhappy "Holy Land", the London Times in its wisdom sought to incite them further: it displayed prominently on its first page a disgraceful quote from a rabbi's racist statement against the Arabs during the funeral of Baruch Goldstein in Israel. There was no call for the display of such "Fleet Street" zealotry. Alas, the UK is for many these days a very unexciting place, governed by a hapless unimpressive government, perhaps the worst government this country has known this century. Excitement is therefore sought vicariously and often immorally at the expense of other people's misfortunes. But this is also, after all, a society of impressive multi-perversion as we approach the end of the millennium.
3. See the epilogue in my recent book, *Among Arabs and Jews, A Personal Experience 1936–1990*, London, Weidenfeld & Nicolson, 1991, pp.142–3.

Peace and Israeli Security

DOV S. ZAKHEIM

YITZHAK RABIN'S 13 September 1993 handshake with Yasir Arafat on the White House lawn has created more hopes for a new and peaceful Middle East than any single event since Anwar Sadat's dramatic trip to Jerusalem 16 years earlier. These hopes range from grand designs for an Israel secure in its role as the economic hub of a Middle Eastern community patterned after the European Union, to expectations that the Israeli defence budget can finally be reduced to more modest proportions. Only time will reveal where Israel actually will stand on the spectrum of visions for its future. Still, it may be possible even today to outline at least the bounds of a realistic security future that is likely to present itself to Israel in the aftermath of a peace agreement.

The following pages will attempt to outline the possibilities for a new security environment for Israel, and its implications for Israeli defence programmes, expenditures and industries. It will assume that, despite setbacks such as the Hebron massacre, Israel will have reached a peace agreement with at least two of its immediate neighbours – Jordan and Syria, as well as an understanding with Syria regarding the status of Lebanon and a consequent agreement with that country, and a workable arrangement with a Palestinian entity. This appraisal will not address the issue of whether that entity will be fully independent or possessed of more limited autonomy, other than to postulate that it will consist of Gaza and much of the West Bank, have its own police force, and maintain full control over its economic affairs.

STRATEGIC SECURITY IN A PEACEFUL ENVIRONMENT: OPPORTUNITIES AND RISKS

The record of Israel's peace with Egypt, now of almost 15 years' duration, provides the most eloquent testimony to the strategic benefits of peace. By virtue of the Camp David Accords, Israel was

Dov S. Zakheim, former Deputy Under-Secretary of Defense in the Reagan Administration, is Chief Executive Officer of SPC International and a Senior Associate of the Center for Strategic and International Studies, Washington, DC.

able to eliminate the largest Arab state from the array of threats it faced. While its military planners always had to consider Egyptian forces as part of any worst-case scenario, their experience during the 1982 war in Lebanon demonstrated that the treaty with Egypt was more durable than many had thought. Despite clear opposition from the Egyptian government to the Israeli thrust northwards, Israel's forces never had to contend with yet another closing of the Suez Canal, or with any major mobilization of Egyptian forces. There was therefore no pressure upon Israel to redeploy any forces away from its northern theatre of operations. Israel was able to prosecute its strategy – for better or for worse – at maximum capacity, without fear of hindrance by Egypt.[1]

Peace with Jordan is likely to have the same military implications as peace with Egypt, although Israel will have to remain ever watchful of the political dynamics in Amman. The Hashemite dynasty has long come to terms with Israel's existence; King Hussein's readiness to sign a peace treaty is in line with his grandfather Abdallah's intention of doing so four decades ago. That Jordan remained out of the conflict with Lebanon, as well as out of the 1973 Yom Kippur war, demonstrates the degree to which Amman has for many years recognized that the benefits of non-belligerence far outweigh the possible domestic political costs of seeming to lack zeal in confronting the Zionist state.

It is therefore not unreasonable to postulate that Jordan is unlikely to enter a war involving Israel and another Arab state, even one of the former "confrontation states", should one or more of them undergo a change of regime or policy. On the contrary, Jordan, as a signatory to a peace treaty, would certainly opt for discretion as the better part of valour and can be expected to remain neutral in any such conflict. Only if the Hashemite regime were to fall, and be replaced by a radical government, possibly a radical Palestinian government, would Israel have to face yet another hostile threat from the East.

Could the Hashemite regime be toppled precisely because it had signed a peace treaty with Israel? There is the example of King Abdallah, who was assassinated for daring to talk to the Israelis, and that of Anwar Sadat, who suffered the same fate for his even greater exertions for peace. On the other hand, King Hussein's attempts to democratize Jordan through the creation of a more active parliament, and thereby to balance hard-line Muslim interests, Palestinian allegiance to his throne, and the tribesmen and military who form his bedrock support, appears to be working.

Moreover, there is no evidence that King Hussein's own personal security precautions have abated, or become any less effective. The greatest threat to his life comes from natural causes, not from disgruntled subjects of whatever variety. It can be expected that the Crown Prince, or another figure identified with the regime, would command the same degree of loyalty from King Hussein's traditional supporters. Among these supporters must be included the government of Israel; in 1970, concern for Hussein's security prompted the Israeli Air Force to intercept Syrian MiG-21 aircraft that threatened to shoot down the royal plane with the King on board.[2] Moreover the economic interests that have led to the peaceful development of the Jordan Valley on both sides of the frontier, and to the eager anticipation of many Jordanian businessmen, scientists and academics for new relationships with Israel, are also unlikely to be altered with the accession of a new monarch.

The Gulf states, including Saudi Arabia, have already made it clear, to a greater or lesser degree, that they welcome peace with Israel. Many leading businessmen in the Gulf view their counterparts in Israel as ideal commercial partners; some, like Adnan Khashoggi, have reportedly already entered into such partnerships. The governments of Kuwait and Saudi Arabia, in announcing that they have lifted the secondary boycott against Israel, have demonstrated that they view peace as a precursor to economic cooperation. Similarly, senior Qatari officials have not been reticent about their discussions with Israeli Energy Minister Moshe Shahal regarding a major gas deal between the two countries.[3] Given their small military forces and commensurately limited capabilities, their record of avoiding recent conflicts with Israel, and the positive business inertia that peace is likely to create, Israeli planners have little reason to expect to face southern Gulf forces in the event of a conflict with another Arab state.

Similar observations simply cannot be applied to Syria, even to a Syria under Hafiz al-Asad that might sign a peace agreement with Israel. Syria is the only one of Israel's neighbours that claims as its patrimony the land that constituted the southern portion of the nineteenth century Turkish provinces of Syria. The geo-strategic rivalry between the two states dates back millennia, to Biblical times. Moreover, the basic economic substructure that, after the Second World War, enabled France and Germany to overcome their centuries-old hatreds is unlikely to be duplicated in the economic relations between Syria and Israel. The economics of the two countries are comparable either in terms of per capita GNP or diversification and depth. Israel's is essentially a developed economy, on a par with several European states. Syria has yet to move out of the ranks of less developed states. Syria provides few, if any, markets of significance to Israel; it offers few products of interest to its southern neighbour. Any kind of economic integration, patterned on the EEC, simply would not be sustainable. Thus, were Israel to find itself at war with another

Arab state, it could not count upon Syria to remain neutral, even if a minority Alawite regime were to remain in power.[4] Israeli planners would have to assume for many years to come that the temptation to rupture a treaty, and capitalize on any Israeli preoccupation with another hostile Arab state, is likely to be too great for Syria to overcome unless adequately deterred by Israel Defence Forces (IDF) prowess.

Although it once served as a staging area for PLO attacks on Israel, and now does the same for Hizballah, Lebanon is unlikely to be a direct threat to Israel in a post-settlement environment. Lebanon avoided entanglement in both the 1967 and 1973 wars; it can be expected to do its utmost to avoid entanglement in a future conflict. Presumably, a settlement would involve the expulsion of Hizballah; otherwise it is difficult to see why Israel would withdraw from south Lebanon.

Nevertheless, Israel would have to continue to allocate some resources directed at its Lebanese neighbour, even if its forces withdraw from the south. Lebanon will always be subject to pressures from – and intervention by – Syria and its forces. As a consequence, Israel would have to continue to hedge against the probability of a northern front united against it if Syria chooses to join another Arab state in a confrontation or conflict with Jerusalem.

The so-called "other Arab state" that could enter into conflict with Israel actually could be one of several. To begin with, Iraq remains hostile to Israel. There is no evidence that its hostility would abate with the departure of Saddam Hussein. Unlike their counterparts in Syria, the Iraqi political, social and economic elites have no Golan to recover, that is, no territorial incentive to come to terms with Israel in the first place, or to accept Israel's peace with other states. The ideological elites in the Iraqi Ba'th party also remain hostile to the Jewish state. It is possible that Iraq might view Israel as an attractive business partner, since the Iraqi economy is potentially one of the largest and most diverse in the Middle East. Israel, however, could also be viewed as a dangerous business competitor, thereby furnishing yet another reason for continuing Iraqi hostility. As long as Iraq remains hostile, or potentially hostile, Israel would have to account for its military prowess. This would incorporate not only its ability to marshal forces in support of other Arab states with which Israel might be at war, but also, at some future time, once again to launch long-range missiles with non-conventional warheads at Israeli targets.

Libya likewise shows no indication of accepting Israel's existence, much less a willingness to make peace. There was much speculation about a "hidden agenda" behind the short-lived 1993 visit of Libyan pilgrims to Israel. Since the visit, which ended with rancour on all sides, Muammar Gaddafi has shown no great desire to come to terms with Israel. He or his successor cannot be dismissed as potential threats, especially in association with other hostile Arabs.

Israeli military planners also cannot fully discount the possibility of a major upheaval within Egypt, Algeria (which could rapidly deploy long-range missiles armed with non-conventional warheads) or Saudi Arabia. While the public manifestations of Muslim political extremism are far greater in the two former states, the potential for a domestic explosion is perhaps equally serious in Saudi Arabia. Riyadh's cash flow problems are unlikely to disappear quickly unless the price of oil rises sharply, and remains higher for a relatively lengthy period. That prospect appears remote, at least in the medium term, especially since at some point soon Iraq might once again be able to export its own oil. Continued cash flow difficulties could force the Saudis to cut back on their cradle-to-grave social programmes. Disappointed social welfare expectations on the part of a large number of Saudis could then be coupled with the undercurrent of religious hostility to the regime (both from Wahhabis who feel that the Royal Family is too dissolute, and from Shi'ites who feel persecuted) to create a lethal threat to the Royal Family. A successor regime in Saudi Arabia, such as in Algeria or Egypt, might then find enmity towards Israel yet again to be an effective rallying cry around which the entire nation might unite.

The aforementioned Arab threats to Israel, even that of Iraq, are likely to remain either latent or relatively small scale in the near and medium term. On the other hand, that of non-Arab Iran is far more serious and immediate, and could well be intensified in the aftermath of a peace settlement. Iran has made no bones about its opposition to the peace process. Moreover, there remains no clear evidence that the mullahs are essentially more moderate today than they were a decade ago. Unlike Iraq, Iran continues to brandish long-range missiles, and is reportedly moving ahead with its nuclear programme. It may be the single most threatening adversary that Israel currently faces.

Peace would bring yet another actor into the Middle East drama, the Palestinians. Boasting no regular armed force, a Palestinian entity would still have the ability clandestinely to arm itself, much as Germany did in the aftermath of the First World War. No Palestinian force would itself be a match for the IDF, but Palestinians bearing small arms, hand-held surface-to-air missiles, and other systems could seriously complicate Israel's defences in the event of a conflict.

Not all Palestinians are likely to accept a peace settlement. Israel would also have to hedge against the possibility of terrorist activities launched from the Palestinian entity that the Palestinian police force may not be able to control. Dealing with such attacks would pose a serious dilemma for Israel. If it conducts hot pursuit operations into the territories under Palestinian authority, it would risk alienating an even larger portion of the Palestinian populace, as well as the governing authorities. Israel may have to intensify its security precautions within its own territories. The counter-terrorist missions of the IDF would certainly not disappear with the emergence of a new Palestinian entity.

One other actor must be considered in any calculation of Israel's post-treaty security requirements: the United States. The US has been the region's most successful peacemaker. It was the United States that brokered the disengagement agreements after the 1973 war. The Camp David Accords are a monument to American tenacity in forcing Israel and Egypt to come to an agreement that both clearly wanted. Since 1979, it has been America that has underwritten those accords both with financial assistance to the two parties, and with its contributions to the multinational force of observers that it created.[5] Finally, it was American pressure and persistence that led to the 1991 Madrid Conference and to the host of meetings that have taken place in its aftermath.

The United States continues to exert maximum efforts to realize a comprehensive peace; without those efforts peace is probably unattainable. The nature and utility of an American post-settlement commitment is a subject of considerable debate, however. To begin with, not all Israelis are convinced that the United States can be a long-term guarantor of the peace. As a respected Israeli analyst notes, "with the US serving as . . . potentially . . . a guarantor of any agreements, a post-settlement Arab–Israeli war could require American military intervention . . . precisely at a time when the US will be cutting back its forces and seeking to avoid extended commitments overseas".[6] Moreover, it is not at all clear that a force of observers, modelled after the Sinai force, could function as effectively in a parcel of land that is one-fifth as wide as the Sinai. Finally, American budget realities render it exceedingly unlikely that the United States will undertake another long-term financial commitment to underwrite another Middle Eastern peace agreement.

There is no doubt that, in the short term, peace would eliminate as threats virtually all of the states that have participated in past wars against Israel. This is no mean development, and would represent a major security breakthrough for a state that has been on a war footing for its entire existence. On the other hand, peace would not entirely remove either the threats facing Israel, or the need for Israel to maintain strong defences. Indeed, nothing could be more dangerous for Israel than a false sense of security, such as that which animated Western Europe prior to the Second World War, or the United States in its immediate aftermath. Nevertheless, whereas in the past Israel reflected its ongoing state of war with its neighbours by structuring its forces primarily to mount offensive operations, it would in the future have to take on a more defensive orientation commensurate with the post-settlement environment. The country's overall force posture is likely therefore to shift from one that, whatever its stated doctrine, was geared to pre-emption, to one similar to America's long-time post-war posture, which emphasizes defence and retaliation. The need for a modern and powerful military establishment is thus unlikely to diminish significantly, or with it, the appetites of military programmes.

PEACE AND ISRAELI DEFENCE EXPENDITURES

During the past ten years, Israel's defence budget has been subject to both internal and external strains. Although this burden was reduced in the 1980s, and was cut again as recently as last year, it still accounts for about 15 per cent of the Gross National Product, a share that is "extremely high by any international comparison".[7] Moreover, pressures for increasing the budget appear to be unyielding. The real cost of Israel's weapons systems continues to rise, as it has elsewhere in the world. Since Israel has acquired many of its major systems, especially aircraft, from the United States, it has experienced the same real cost growth (for aircraft, an increase of approximately six per cent compounded annually) that has affected American procurement budgets.[8] In addition, again as with the United States, Israel has experienced growth in wages and support activities that has eaten into procurement, research and development costs as defence budget allocations have been reduced.[9]

At the same time, American military grant aid for Israel has been held constant at $1.8 billion since 1985, resulting in an annual real decline due to inflation. To be sure, other arrangements, such as the funding of the Arrow missile, have to some extent offset that decline. Nevertheless, the overall impact of the ceiling on the security assistance account has added new strains to the defence budget, with no obvious relief in sight.

In an ideal world, Israel could hope to reap a "peace dividend" as a result of an Arab–Israeli settlement. Yet the post-settlement environment is likely to have a greater impact on the nature of defences, not on the resources required to support them. Indeed, it is arguable that a strategy that emphasizes deterrence through defence and retaliation could be more demanding than one emphasizing the threat of pre-emption and war-fighting, for, in addition to the offensive systems required to prosecute a conflict to its successful conclusion, Israel would also need defensive systems to ensure the viability of its force structure in the face of an adversary's initial attack.

Nowhere is this change of posture, and consequently of budgetary need, more evident than in the case of Israel's proposed response to threats from ballistic missiles with non-conventional warheads. As late as 1990, Israel's basic strategy for dealing with the theatre missile threat relied heavily upon the tried and true doctrine of offensive pre-emption by the Israeli Air Force. It was felt that if such missiles posed a threat at all – and many military people argued that they did not – then the Israeli Air Force would locate and destroy their launchers on the ground before a shot could be fired. Moreover, the IDF clearly believed that no one would test Israel's retaliatory might by pre-emptively firing such missiles.[10]

The Scud attacks on Israel during the Gulf War demonstrated the bankruptcy of Jerusalem's strategy. Israel huffed and puffed prior to the war, but its threats to retaliate against Iraq if it were to launch a missile attack fell on deaf ears. Nor did they materialize once the Scuds were fired.[11] Clearly, Israel required a defensive capability in addition to its offensive prowess. The deployment of Patriots helped to some degree in this regard, but the government concluded that it would also have to press ahead with its own longer-range system, the Arrow, towards which its attitude had been rather lukewarm prior to the war.

Arrow clearly constitutes a critical requirement for any Israeli post-settlement defence posture. Together with improvements to the Patriots already acquired by Israel, it could serve as a last-ditch defence against incoming ballistic missiles, whose accuracy would undoubtedly improve with the passage of time. Were Israel to field the Arrow, it would also bolster the credibility of the Israeli deterrent. A potential aggressor – Iran, Iraq or Libya, for example – would have to consider that not only would attacking ballistic missiles fail to reach their targets, but Israeli offensive capabilities, still intact after the attack, would be free to prosecute retaliatory missions.

Arrow's cost would have a major impact upon the ability of the IDF to acquire other needed military capabilities, however. Although the Israeli government has formally classified the programme's costs, a variety of unofficial estimates reveal that the price of the Arrow system is both very high and growing. The original estimates of the Israel Aircraft Industry (IAI) for both development and deployment of the missile and its launchers totalled 1.3 billion (1989) dollars, or about 1.5 billion in 1994 dollars.[12] Historically such early estimates tend to be far lower than actual costs. This appears to be the case with the Arrow as well. The value of the Arrow development contracts alone now amounts to 534 million in 1994 dollars.[13] The most recent procurement estimates, excluding development, now total slightly over $1.3 billion. Thus, that portion of the programme associated with the missiles and launchers has experienced approximately 20 per cent cost real growth in five years.

Moreover, the procurement figures do not account for the cost of acquisition radars, fire control radars, and command and control, and support costs for operating the missile, all of which are separate Israeli budget line items. When added to the missile and launcher costs, the totals approach 4.5 billion 1994 dollars.[14] This is a huge sum, which still does not account for future cost growth due to a variety of developments, including concurrency in developing the radars and the missile system, technical difficulties and the limitations of Israel's cost estimating approach.[15]

To be sure, the missile development programme is being funded virtually in its entirety by the United States. Some of those funds, however, are drawn from the Offshore Procurement Programme, and are being applied therefore to Arrow directly at the expense of other Israeli programmes. In addition, all other Arrow-related development programmes are being funded by Israel itself, while procurement, likewise, is unlikely to be funded by the United States. These outlays would therefore come at the expense of other Israeli programmes.

Arrow is not the only system whose acquisition is rendered even more important in a post-settlement Middle East, however. Israel's recent purchase of 20 long-range F-15I strike aircraft likewise takes on new importance as a deterrent against those very same long-range missiles against which Israel must defend. Like Arrow, the F-15I purchase represents a major financial undertaking for Israel. Its cost is estimated to total $2.05 billion, and has yet to be finalized, as would the mode of financing an Israeli budget shortfall of $250 million, and this could result in reductions in funding for other programmes.[16]

Israel must also modernize its Merkava force; the Gulf War demonstrated that however effective modern munitions might be, there was still a major role for armour to play in the Middle Eastern environment. Even if plans for a new Merkava 4 force remain frozen, there would still be a need to upgrade current Merkava 3 systems. In addition, there are some 600 smaller projects designed to improve the fire-power of artillery and the survivability of armoured vehicles.[17]

Israel is also in the midst of a major naval modernization programme. Its longer-range corvettes and submarines constitute another retaliatory capability against distant foes launching ballistic missiles against Israeli targets. In addition, Israel appears committed to expanding its space programme, both with respect to communications as well as in terms of its long-range missile-launcher and satellite capability.

Finally, Israel would have to pay greater attention, and more money, to operations and services (O&S), an area that appears to have been neglected somewhat in recent years, resulting in shortfalls in stocks and training time.[18] In the past decade, the operations and services accounts have witnessed what have been termed "inflated" increases in wages and service conditions, leading to a more "hollow" force.[19] Some efficiencies might be realized in the O&S accounts through tighter budget control and programmes such as Total Quality Management.[20] There are limits to the savings such programmes can generate, however, and, at least in past American experience, they have always promised much more than they actually delivered. Efficiencies would not obviate the need for more O&S spending, which would no doubt come at the expense of weapons development and procurement.

Some savings are, of course, possible. A peaceful resolution of the dispute with the Palestinians should reduce that part of the defence budget related to combatting the *intifada*. The length of active duty service requirement might be further reduced, freeing Israelis to attend university or enter the workforce at a younger age. Reserve obligations may also be reduced even more than in the recent past, resulting in fewer disruptions to the peacetime economy. In both cases, training budgets could be lowered somewhat. On the other hand, Israel would have to find the resources to relocate facilities from areas previously occupied to territories remaining under its control.[21] The United States, or some other powers, might be persuaded to help cover the relocation costs, much as the US funded the construction of air bases in the Negev after the Sinai withdrawal. Claims upon the aid budgets of all Western states have been increasing, however, due to the needs of Eastern Europe, the former Soviet Union, and the prospective requirements of the Palestinians. It is unclear to what extent Israel could successfully compete with these new claimants for a larger slice of the American aid pie, or for any slice of the European one.

Another potential source of budget reductions could be arms control. Since 29 May 1991, when President George Bush launched his post-Gulf War arms control initiative, considerable attention has been paid to the prospects of limiting both non-conventional and conventional weapons in the Middle East. Some small degree of progress has been achieved: the United Nations has created a register for arms sales, and in 1993 Israel signed the international chemical weapons convention and agreed to join the Missile Technology Control Regime (MTCR).

In practical terms, however, little appears to have changed. A post-settlement Middle East might be more likely to tolerate some degree of arms control and/or reduction. It would be in the interests of all parties to reduce the size of their hedges against a rupture of the peace in order to realize budgetary savings. Enforceable agreements to eliminate the development of weapons of mass destruction and their delivery systems may be more easily attainable than they are today. On the other hand, the ongoing opposition of several states to a Middle East settlement, some of which, such as Iran, are believed to have advanced nuclear and other non-conventional programmes,[22] would constrain Israel's willingness to reduce its armaments levels, or the degree of their modernization. Israel would only do so if the rejectionists are equally willing to submit to constraints, which would seem most unlikely. For similar reasons, Israel may still be reluctant to enter into any further agreements that might constrain its ability to field non-conventional weaponry.

Indeed, even some of Israel's Arab neighbours might find themselves unable to accept arms control proposals not because of their fear of Israel, but due to their fear of other neighbours. Syrian concerns regarding Turkey, and Saudi concerns about Iran and Iraq are but two cases in point. Certainly, in the three years since Bush first outlined his proposals, the Middle East has continued to absorb very large quantities of armaments, including major Israeli and Saudi aircraft purchases from the United States. Arms control may therefore prove almost as difficult in the post-settlement era as it was prior to September 1993.

Some Israeli observers argue that peace should bring about the transformation of the Israeli military into what former Chief of Staff Dan Shomron called a "small, smart army".[23] Such a force would only be realized in the long term, if at all. Even a move away from heavy armour, and its replacement by an emphasis on sophisticated munitions capable of being delivered at long ranges, would not necessarily result in defence budget reductions. In sum, the need to cope with longer-range threats in a post- settlement environment, coupled with the need to hedge against a possible change of regime in states at peace with Israel, would ensure that a "peace dividend" for Israel simply would not materialize any time soon.

THE DEFENCE INDUSTRIAL SECTOR AFTER A SETTLEMENT

Peace would enable Israel to expand its export market for armaments, without which its domestic industry may only be able to survive at a cost to the defence budget that any government might find intolerable.[24] Israel is among the world's leaders in the production of sophisticated military electronics, smaller systems such as missiles and unmanned aerial vehicles, and the conversion and upgrade of older weapons. The latter capability is of particular interest to states that formerly relied on the Soviet Union for their weapons supplies.

The prospect of Middle East peace has already opened up new markets in Eastern Europe and the former Soviet Union, and these can be expected to expand in future years. Markets in the Far East, notably in Japan and Korea, and some of the ASEAN states, once off-limits to Israel as a result of the Arab boycott, can be expected likewise to become open to Israel's armaments industries just as they are beginning to open in other sectors. In some cases, the transition from a long-standing clandestine sales relationship to an open one is also likely to result in increased exports, as is apparently the case with respect to China.

Peace would also increase the prospects for more indirect sales to Arab states, and possibly some direct ones. Israel has long exported some of its defence products to the Arabs as a sub-contractor on American programmes. Direct sales, at least of non-lethal equipment, can be anticipated to states such as those in the Gulf. They are unlikely to have any incentive to enter into hostilities with Israel, even if it were to become embroiled in a conflict with rejectionist states or former enemies again turned hostile.

The emergence of new markets for Israeli military exports is of crucial importance, because Israel's largest market in this sector, the United States, has entered a period of steep budgetary decline. The Defense Department's new emphasis on research in favour of acquisition limits the prospects for all foreign manufacturers, including Israel's, to sell their developed wares to the American military. Although it might be argued that constrained defence budgets should prompt American purchases of foreign equipment in order to obtain the most efficient returns on its defence expenditures, there is little concrete evidence to support such a hypothesis. Indeed, it is possible that a desire to protect American jobs would lead to further downturns in American purchases from abroad. The failure of American two-way street programmes in the later 1980s testifies to the American propensity to erect new, more subtle barriers to foreign purchases when diminished budgets threaten the prospects of domestic producers.

Any increase in Israel's weapons exports would have a salutary effect on its own defence budgets. As a result of greater economies of scale, overheads could be spread more widely, and the unit costs of systems would be reduced. The government would thus be in a position to acquire more needed systems, or indeed, to reduce the defence budgets. To that extent, Israel might actually realize a financial peace dividend after all.

CONCLUSION

There can be no denying that peace is in Israel's interest. Peace can only bring benefits to a nation that is weary of losing its sons (and daughters) on countless battlefields. Whether peace can be sustained, is, however, a rather different matter. To increase the prospects that peace would endure, Israel would be required to maintain a strong military posture. That posture would of necessity have to account not only for threats from states unwilling to subscribe to a settlement at all, but those that might renege on it. To do so, and not appear to be unnecessarily belligerent in a post-settlement environment, would demand that Israel expend considerable resources to support a strategy of deterrence, defence and retaliation at both shorter and longer range. The magnitude of resources required is likely to wipe out any chance of a peace dividend, other than that which might be realized through increased military sales abroad. While the United States may be expected to exert maximal efforts to achieve a settlement, its ability to finance that settlement, or to increase its budgetary commitments to Israel is highly uncertain. Israel would have to seek more internal efficiencies than it has found so far, and would have to make some very painful choices among weapons programmes. That, however, remains a small price to pay for obtaining what Israel has sought since its birth: a reduced threat of war and therefore, a far less stressful existence for all its citizens.

NOTES

1. It is noteworthy that Chaim Herzog, in his excellent chapter on the War in Lebanon, does not mention Egypt even once. See Chaim Herzog, *The Arab-Israeli Wars*, revised edition, New York, Vintage, 1984. Egypt does not figure in Ze'ev Schiff and Ehud Ya'ari's account of the war either, apart from a brief reference to Egypt's provision to Arafat of intelligence regarding the IDF's war preparations. See Ze'ev Schiff and Ehud Ya'ari, *Israel's Lebanon War* (trans. Ina Friedman), New York, Simon & Schuster, 1984, p.78.
2. The claim was made by former Israeli Air Force Commander, Maj.-General (res.) Mordecai Hod to *Agence France Presse*; AFP, "Former Air Force Head Saved Jordan's Hussein", 9 June 1993.
3. See Dov S. Zakheim, "Persian Gulf Off the Screen", *Washington Times*, 30 Jan. 1994, p.B4.
4. The Alawites, long viewed by the Sunni majority as a heretical Muslim sect (despite a *fatwa* issued by a Lebanese Shi'ite mullah allied politically to Asad), are also widely known to have supported the Jewish settlers in mandatory Palestine. See Daniel Pipes, *Damascus Courts the West: Syrian Politics, 1989–1991*, Washington, DC, The Washington Institute, 1991, p.8 and endnote 10.
5. See William B. Quandt, *The Peace Process: American Diplomacy and the Arab–Israeli Conflict Since 1967*, Washington, DC, Brookings, 1993, p.341.
6. Dore Gold, *Fundamental Factors in a Stabilized Middle East: Security, Territory, and Peace*, Washington, DC, Jewish Institute for National Security Affairs, 1993, p.17.
7. Nadav Halevi, "Economic Implications of Peace: The Israeli Perspective", paper delivered at the conference on "The Economics of Middle East Peace", Institute for Social and Economic Policy in the Middle East, John F. Kennedy School of Government, Harvard University, 14–16 Nov. 1991, pp.16–17.
8. See Dov S. Zakheim and Jeffrey M. Ranney, "Matching Defense Strategies to Resources: Challenges for the Clinton Administration", *International Security*, Vol.18 (Summer 1993), p.67.
9. Aluf Ben, "The Limits of Authority", *Ha'aretz*, 30 May 1993, p.B1.
10. For a complete discussion see Reuven Pedhatzur, *Ma'arechet Ha'chetz Ve'hahagana Ha'activit Neged Tilim Balisti'im: Etgarim U'sheelot* ("The Arrow System and Active Defence Against Ballistic Missiles: Challenges and Issues"), Tel-Aviv, Jaffee Centre for Strategic Studies, 1993, pp.2–4.
11. Ibid., pp.9–10.
12. Pedhatzur, *Maarechet*, pp.47–8. The 1994 estimate employs Department of Defense inflation factors for outlays in the procurement accounts.

13. The US General Accounting Office has recently reported that the total cost of Arrow and ACES (the Arrow follow-on programme) development contracts is $518.3 million. See US General Accounting Office, *US–Israel Arrow/ACES Program: Cost, Technical, Proliferation, and Management Concerns*, Washington, DC, GPO, 1993, pp.2–5. This article inflates the GAO figures using DoD inflation factors for procurement; it assumes that all Arrow costs were based on 1989 dollar values, while all ACES costs were based on 1991 dollar values, that is, the respective years in which the Arrow and ACES contracts were signed.

14. Derived from ibid., pp.47–8. These estimates also fall well within the range of those presented by Marvin Feuerwerger, a former Defense Department official who served in Israel. His 1991 estimate of between $2 and $5 billion was not normalized to constant dollars. See Marvin Feuerwerger, *The Arrow Next Time? Israel's Missile Defense Program for the 1990s*, Washington, DC, The Washington Institute, 1991, pp.28–30.

15. GAO, *US–Israel Arrow/ACES Program*, p.4. It is noteworthy that just three months after the release of the GAO report, the US Army reported an increase in its portion of the Arrow programme totalling $9.3 million for risk reduction modifications. See Joseph Lovece, "More Cost Growth: Israeli Arrow Missile's 'Eyes' Boost Project Price Another $5 Million", *Defense Week*, 12 July 1993, p.6.

16. Craig A. Rasmussen, "Israel Looks at Financing Options for F-15 Buy: May Have to Delay Purchase of Blackhawks, MLRS", *Inside the Pentagon*, 3 Feb. 1994, p.3.

17. Aluf Ben, "The Era of the Small, Smart Army Has Not Yet Arrived", *Ha'aretz*, 25 April 1993, p.B3.

18. Ibid.

19. Aluf Ben, "The Limits of Authority", *Ha'aretz*, 30 May 1993, p.B1.

20. Amy Dockser Marcus, "Israeli Military Tries Total Quality Management to Make the Most of a Small Army and Budgets", *Wall Street Journal*, 24 Aug. 1993, p.6.

21. Halevi, *Economic Implications of Peace*, p.19.

22. For a brief discussion, see Geoffrey Kemp, with Shelley A. Stahl, *The Control of the Middle East Arms Race*, Washington, DC, Carnegie Endowment for International Peace, 1991, pp.71–5.

23. Ben, *Small, Smart Army*, p.B3.

24. The export market is critical to Israel's armaments industry. For example, exports by Israel Aircraft Industries, the largest company in the state and its largest exporter, accounted for nearly 77 per cent of all sales in 1992. See Aluf Ben, "The Aircraft Industry Has Lost Its Ability to Compete", *Ha'aretz*, 14 July 1993, p.C1.

The Diaspora and the Peace Process

MAX BELOFF

T HE "PEACE PROCESS" under consideration was that launched by President Bush and President Gorbachev at the Madrid Conference opened on 30 October 1991, which was rescued from stalemate by secret negotiations in Norway during the summer of 1993 and proclaimed to the world as destined for success by the Rabin–Arafat handshake on the White House lawn on 13 September 1993. At the time of writing (shortly after the signing of the May 1994 agreement on the implementation of the Washington accords), the process is still remote from its goal and the future is still uncertain. Yet it has already illuminated the present state of relations between Israel and the Jewish diaspora and perhaps contributed to altering them in the future.

It can be seen that this was bound to be the case since the issues raised by the peace process particularly where the Palestinian side of it was concerned were deeply embedded in the history of Zionism. Many of the problems had been confronted by that movement's leaders both inside and outside mandatory Palestine before the creation of the State, especially in relation to the "partition" proposals of the late 1930s and again in the immediately post-war years.

Israel is not the only country to have an active diaspora, directing its attention to the doings of the country with which it identifies on historical or religious grounds. The Irish and Armenians come to mind as long-standing examples of a relationship of this kind. What is unique about Israel is that the homeland in its modern guise has been created by a calling back of the descendants of the original exiles. However concerned Americans or Australians of Irish descent may be with the politics of Ireland, however willing to put words or money into the causes they uphold there, they do not intend to make it their home. Members of such diasporas believe that they can find an acceptable future in the countries where they live and in which they are only

Lord Beloff, FBA, is Emeritus Professor of Government and Public Administration at Oxford University.

examples of a number of ethnic groups nearly all of them non-indigenous which have made their home there.

The Zionist credo was that such coexistence was not in the long run tenable or, in another version, would only be tenable if the Jews of the diaspora could look also to a state of their own. Zionist leaders had both to proclaim the attractions of a return to the original homeland and to emphasize the probability that events outside it might eventually force those originally reluctant to accept their message to realize that they had no other option. Since when the message was launched sovereignty over the Jewish homeland was in other hands, the Zionist leaders were driven to follow the path of international diplomacy to bring about their goal and to take what advantage they could of the rivalries between the great powers for influence in the region. In that respect the political leaders of Israel are subject to the same constraints.

The nearest parallel to the Jewish diaspora is ironically the Palestinian diaspora consisting of those who were driven out of or fled Israel at the time of the War of Independence or who left the occupied territories after the war of 1967 and the descendants of both groups.[1] Like many Jews in the diaspora many Palestinians who have made a life elsewhere will want to remain where they are. Others will want to return to or seek a new life in the Palestinian State or whatever other entity evolves in the West Bank and Gaza. Some will no doubt continue to press for a return to their families' original roots in Israel itself.

One of the main difficulties that have confronted all attempts at a peaceful settlement of the Arab–Israeli dispute including the present "peace process" has been the difficulty that Israelis and Palestinians have in understanding the reality of each other's nationalism. Yet although their histories have been very different, the original source of both their ideologies was the European nineteenth-century development of the idea that the nation-state is now the only acceptable form of political organization and the only one to have complete legitimacy.

The founders of Zionism did not need to define the nation which they proposed to endow with statehood. Two millennia of experience in the western world had placed the Jews in a situation in which their own self-image and collective institutions were the consequence of their religious separation from the people among whom they lived. It is true that while the original form of discrimination against the Jews was based on religious grounds, the reaction against them after emancipation and their entry into general society was also based on racial arguments. In Britain the opposition to Disraeli's pro-Turkish foreign policy in 1876–80 was fuelled by the assertion that despite his adherence to the established church, he was swayed by his Jewish affinities, preferring the relative tolerance of the Turks to the anti-Jewish policies of the Balkan Slavs and their Russian protectors.[2] The later anti-

semitism in western and central Europe that reached its apotheosis in
the Nazi doctrine was almost everywhere expressed in racial terms
with the partial exception of France where, as was proved during the
Vichy regime, the Catholic Church carried on the age-old battle of
Church versus synagogue.

When after the creation of the State of Israel it became a refuge also
for Jews from what had been the Ottoman Empire, the environment
with which they were familiar was one in which individuals were
grouped and classified and treated according to their religious adherence.
Yet at the same time, there was in Israel as there had been in the diaspora
a large number of Jews who interpreted the idea of a "Jewish State" as
not necessarily involving a religious connotation. In that sense the
definition of Jewish nationalism is more complicated than in the case of
the familiar European examples; it necessitated the development of
Hebrew as a living language, a feat that only the Irish have tried to
emulate with their historic tongue, and in their case unsuccessfully.

The development of Palestinian nationalism was complex in a
different way. Its emergence was part of a general growth in Arab self-
consciousness during the declining years of the Ottoman Empire as a
whole, and when the future of the area was settled by external powers
after that Empire's defeat and collapse at the end of the First World War
it was not a definitive one. And to some degree the original uncertainty
remains. Some potential nation-states emerged: Egypt, Syria, Lebanon,
Iraq were joined after the Second World War by Jordan and the
countries of the Maghreb. New sovereign entities emerged in the
Arabian Peninsula itself. But it was an open question whether the
ultimate goal was some pan-Arab or pan-Islamic destiny or whether
the European nation-state should remain the model. The question was
complicated by the divisions in Islam and in some Arab countries by
the presence of sizeable and important Christian minorities. For the
Palestinians themselves, Damascus and Baghdad represented alternative focal points and placed their diplomacy in a situation not so different
from that of the Zionist leadership before 1914.

From both the Palestinian and the Israeli point of view, a particular
problem was presented by what became the kingdom of Jordan. In the
inter-allied negotiations during the First World War this territory was
assigned to the British sphere of influence and thus in Jewish eyes was
covered by the Balfour Declaration. Some Zionist ambitions went
even further. "The fathers of Zionism", writes one authority, "sought
a greater Israel that included most of Transjordan and parts of Lebanon
and Syria." The same writer argues that it was easier for the Zionist
leaders ultimately to accept a narrower definition of the national home
because their views were not directly affected by religious considerations. In more recent years we have witnessed both in Israel and in the

diaspora the emergence of religious parties and associations whose
agenda is a political one.[3]

Britain from the beginning of the mandate ruled out Transjordan as
a potential area for Jewish settlement and gave it a separate existence
under the Hashemite dynasty which barred access to Jews. After taking
part in the invasion of Israel following the British withdrawal, Jordan
found itself in possession of the West Bank including the old city of
Jerusalem. At the same time it became a home to many Palestinians
whose numbers were increased by a further influx after the 1967 War.
Jordan thus became a country the majority of whose inhabitants were
Palestinians, although power remained with the dynasty and its local
adherents. Relations between Israel and Jordan were thus conditioned
by the internal politics of both countries, neither wishing to see an
independent Palestinian entity established, and up to 1967, more or less
covert diplomatic contacts helped to retain the *status quo*.[4]

When in 1967 most of the territory that had been held by Jordan was
conquered by Israel, many Israeli politicians continued to believe that
the only alternative to direct rule which was certain to be burdensome
was some kind of arrangement with Jordan. On the other hand, the
Palestinians in Jordan shared with those under occupation the ambition
for a Palestinian state covering all mandatory Palestine. Thus at the
time of the 1991 Gulf War when Yasir Arafat upheld the cause of
Saddam Hussein, Jordan went along with this policy much to its
own economic detriment. Since then it has appeared resigned to the
emergence of some kind of Palestinian political entity in some kind of
confederation or association with itself.

In Israel itself some elements on the right have argued that since the
Palestinians already have a state, namely Jordan, they do not require
the West Bank – Judea and Samaria – which for them is an integral part
of *Eretz Israel*. The "Jordan is Palestine" slogan also has, like most
Israeli positions, adherents in the diaspora. Others have gone further
and advocated the expulsion into Jordan of the entire Arab populations
of the West Bank.

Despite the presence of large numbers of Palestinian Arabs both in the
West Bank and Gaza and in Israel itself, the Palestinian diaspora has so
far had to operate on the earlier Zionist model, being largely devoted to
fund-raising to keep its institutions in being. But it has also played a part
in countering pro-Israeli sentiments and in directing pro-Palestinian
propaganda at foreign governments. In both Houses of the British
Parliament discussions of the peace process tend to reproduce the
official positions of the Israeli government and the PLO, with few or
no reservations.

The problem for the PLO in respect of the peace process has been in
part the coming to terms with the internal leadership of the Palestinians.

The role of the Jewish diaspora has been at least as complex. Future historians may take the view that what made the idea of a peaceful solution to the Arab–Israeli conflict possible was one internal and one external change in the situation. Internally it appeared that the PLO leadership had given up hope of getting its way by force. The *intifada* had produced victims but not victories. Externally it had become clear that for the foreseeable future, there was no prospect of the Russians intervening on the Arab side. The United States, Israel's patron, had shown its dominant position in the region in the Gulf War. Gorbachev's co-sponsorship of the Madrid Conference (just before the collapse of his own authority and of the Soviet Union itself) was no more than a permitted face-saving gesture.

Since the United States had already after "Suez" seen the elimination of any serious competition in the Middle East from the British or the French, the core question in any study of the diaspora's impact must largely be a matter of looking at American Jewry.

It was for long an article of faith in the British Foreign Office, going back to the time of Ernest Bevin but not confined to anti-semites, that United States policy in the area was to be explained wholly in terms of the influence of the "Jewish lobby" with successive American Presidents and, above all, with Congress. Americans who have taken a different line to that of their government are prone to confirm this view.[5]

Whatever credence we attach to this claim, the fact that it can be advocated shows how distant we are from the days when the international aspect of implementing the Zionist idea first came to the fore. We have a different diaspora. The background to the original Zionist diplomacy was almost exclusively European. American Jewry's involvement was relatively unimportant before the First World War; and even during the inter-war period when some American Jews played a leading role, the leadership of the movement remained firmly European including in this designation the leaders of the Jewish community in Palestine (the *Yishuv*).

In Herzl's time the European diaspora was itself deeply divided. Most Jews living in western Europe were more concerned with their relations with their host communities than with aspirations to a separate national identity. Indeed the Zionists encountered much antagonism, especially among the more established Jews, because it seemed to call in question their right to be regarded as having allegiance only to their countries of residence and citizenship. On the other hand, the pressure exercised upon the Jews of Russia and Romania was such as to make plausible the Zionist claim that their only hope lay in emigration. Most in fact emigrated to the United States or elsewhere in the West; but some were pulled by ideology to choose Israel. And even among the majority of those who migrated to the West, ideas and aspirations nurtured in the Russian Empire came in their baggage. Zionism in western Europe and the United States between the wars was largely an affair of the *Ostjüden*.

The position was radically changed by the Holocaust which eliminated the heartland of European Jewry. During the post-war years, the remnants of East European Jewry outside the boundaries of the Soviet Union found their way either to Israel or to the United States. Western European Jewry in Germany, the Low Countries, France and Italy also largely disappeared as a result of the Holocaust. In France, the numerical losses were made up after the coming of Algerian independence by an influx from North Africa, so that only in Britain and France were Jews numerous enough to play a meaningful part in the external relations of Israel.

A much larger Jewish element survived in the Soviet Union. Since restrictions on emigration remained almost insurmountable, Israel represented a distant hope rather than a living reality. With the lightening of these restrictions in the 1980s there came about a massive change. Of those who left most found their way to Israel as being the only country that placed no obstacles to their immigration, though for a proportion it was seen as only a temporary place of asylum on the way to what were seen as the greater personal opportunities offered by the United States. While the pace of emigration from what was the Soviet Union has been subject to considerable fluctuation in response to changing economic and political conditions, it is the impact on Israel itself that has to be reassessed from time to time rather than any interplay between the diaspora itself and Israeli policy. In none of the countries that were once part of the Soviet Union are Jews in a strong enough position to influence the policies of their governments and with the growth of anti-semitism in many of them they would be unwise to try.

Another vanished element of the diaspora has been the Jewry of the Arab world. The few Jews who have remained in Arab countries have been hostages rather than participants in the Arab–Israeli dialogue. One could argue that an exception must be made for the Jewish inhabitants of the Maghreb who have retreated to France. For the leadership of the Jewish community in France has now largely passed to them and France remains of some importance in Middle Eastern affairs. We have seen the shift from the pro-Israel attitudes of the Fourth Republic to the largely anti-Israel attitudes of the Fifth Republic which are the more significant in the light of France's permanent membership of the Security Council. Yet it is unlikely that France's Jewish community can have much weight either with the French government or indeed with Israel. It must largely be concerned with a defensive role in a country where ethnic tensions have been exacerbated by the presence of a large Islamic minority also the product of France's abandonment of its North African empire.

The changes in the composition of the world Jewry thus briefly outlined help to explain a statistical change over the century now approaching its close. Current reckoning would suggest that there are about 4.2 million Jews in Israel; 5.8 million in North America and about 3 million in the rest of the world.[6] But these figures have not stabilized. Israel's own population will go on increasing through immigration mainly from the former Soviet Union but probably from other quarters as well – South Africa, Latin America?

On the other hand the size of the North American community is likely to diminish as a result of assimilation.[7] And the same may be true of the United Kingdom. All this suggests that, barring some catastrophe, by the end of the century most Jews recognizable as such will be living in Israel and two millennia of history will have been reversed.

While such long-term trends must be taken into account, political leaders both in Israel and the diaspora have to take into account the immediate problems they confront and the attitudes towards them of those they purport to lead. It was certainly the case that American Jews played some part in securing the support of the United States government for the recognition by the United Nations of the State of Israel. But the problems created by the coming into being of the State and the hostility towards it of its neighbours were not perhaps immediately taken in. It has been powerfully argued that the real turning point was the 1967 Six Day War and the perception it created throughout the diaspora of a real threat to Israel's existence, and this was particularly true of the United States:

> Israel became far more prominent in Jewish diaspora life. Several commentators were moved to say that Israel had become the religion of American Jews. A new activism began to permeate world Jewry. Jews were to be found less often praying to God than raising funds, mobilizing support, and engaging in political lobbying on behalf of Israel or Soviet Jewry or the fight against anti-semitism.[8]

In so far as Israel was central to Jewish concerns, the situation was more complicated than at first sight appeared. As a prominent Israeli scholar has pointed out:

> Israel projects to the world a global national understanding of Jewish identity based upon a common culture, a civilization. It demands that Jewish communities in the diaspora accept this as a

normative ideal. But inside Israel two kinds of identities are developing, one radically assimilationist and the other segregationist. Both identities, it is worth noting, originated in the diaspora.[9]

Rival conceptions of the national identity are relevant to Israel's own attitude towards the peace process but they also have the effect both in Israel and in the diaspora "towards a preoccupation with domestic agendas".[10] If diaspora communities are becoming mainly concerned with their domestic problems – paying for their religious and educational institutions and fighting anti-semitism, will they have time to devote to understanding the fast moving scene in Israel or the energy to play a role in the reshaping of its relations with its neighbours?

Hitherto one important role of the diaspora in countries where Jews had money and were free to use it was to give material support both to Israel's general development and to particular public services there, notably in health and higher education. They could also through financial support give assistance to particular aspects of *aliya*. The proportion of a given community's philanthropic effort that went to Israel was one index of Israel's centrality to its concerns. So that when it was recently revealed that there had been a substantial decrease in the proportion of funds collected from American Jews that was going to Israel – now about 30 per cent of the total – it was felt to be an index of the degree to which the most important element in the diaspora had become inward-looking and self-regarding.[11]

Of more direct relevance to our present inquiry has been the degree to which diaspora communities have brought pressure to bear on their own governments in favour of Israeli positions. Pressures in favour of their co-religionists abroad had long figured in the activities of emancipated Jewries in western Europe and North America.[12] But it was always assumed that such activity was compatible with total allegiance to their country of citizenship. The argument against Zionism put by many of the notables in these communities was that if a Jewish State did come into being, the question of a double allegiance would be raised and lend credence to anti-semitism in its political version. The issue was not an abstract one in the case of major countries whose own national interests were involved in the Middle East. Zionists also had to endeavour to prove that their concerns were fully compatible with the national interests of the governments they hoped to win to their cause. From one point of view, the Balfour Declaration itself could be seen as a triumph for Zionist leaders based in the allied countries over their German counterparts.[13]

Difficult questions only arise when a particular Jewish concern runs counter to the host government's view of the national interest. Jewish leaders have been divided on whether in such cases to observe a low profile or risk accusations of "double allegiance" and so give comfort to the anti-semites. It was a dilemma that faced British Jews in Bevin's time and was made more acute by the fact that the most prominent Jews on the political scene were identified with the Labour Party. The Labour Party's attitude to "Suez" involved a renewal of such uncertainties. More recently when the weight of Jewish electoral support and the weight of Jewish membership in the House of Commons have shifted to the Conservatives, anxieties have been expressed about the degree to which communal leaders have played down the comparatively supine attitude of the British government towards the Arab boycott.

Party as well as national allegiances are bound to affect Jewish behaviour. The fact that American Jews have been largely identified with the Democratic Party and the press by and large supports it, is by no means irrelevant to their handling of foreign policy issues including those affecting Israel.[14] On the other hand there was until the beginning of the "peace process" a degree of consistency in relations between the United States and Israel to which the input of American Jews was secondary. It was assumed that Israel was the most reliable cold war ally of the United States in the Middle East. And this justified both a benevolent attitude towards the transfer of funds from American Jews to Israel and direct government-to-government assistance, notably in military matters.

Since the United States had clients in the Arab world as well – notably Saudi Arabia – there were however occasions when Jewish pressure was mobilized to prevent arms supplies to them from menacing Israel's security. Israel's abstention from intervention in the Gulf War despite the provocation of Iraq's missile attacks so as not to hamper the Untied States in maintaining its coalition with other Arab countries was a testimony to the realism with which Israel's statesmen viewed their relationship with the United States.

In respect of Israel's own relations with its neighbours including the Palestinians, the attitude of American Jewry was no different from that of other Jewish communities in the West. The same divisions between "left" and "right" – "doves" and "hawks" were to be found among them as existed in Israel itself. But by and large their instinct was to echo the positions of the government of the day in Israel whatever its political complexion.

The change as far as the United States was concerned came with the running down of the cold war and the seeming determination of the United States to use its advantage to bring about an end to the Arab–Israeli struggle and so minimize one area of overseas commitment. The question was the degree of pressure the United States would be willing to exert on all sides and how American Jewry would react to such pressure as was likely to be put on Israel. The precedent of the Camp David Accords suggested that US intervention could achieve a good deal but much had happened since Begin's settlement with Sadat, notably the Lebanon War and Israel's presence in southern Lebanon. Reagan and then Bush and after him Clinton faced a new situation on both sides of the conflict.

Much has changed also in the attitudes of American Jewry in the more than a quarter of a century that has elapsed since the 1967 War. The centrality of Israel in its concerns has diminished. For one thing, while there has been some immigration to Israel from the United States it is not numerically of great significance. Nor have the changes brought about in Israel by other aspects of immigration and the mere lapse of time deepened their sense of identification with it. The Jewish vision of most American Jews is fixed on their inherited memories of east European Jewry, now a vanished world. To them contemporary Israel looks like a part of a Mediterranean or even Middle Eastern world – Levantine in the opprobrious sense of the word and with that world they have no natural rapport save the religious one which has ceased to be of overwhelming significance. Middle-class Jews in the United States do not encourage their children to make *aliya*. They may think it a good idea for them to go for a year to sample *kibbutz* life or to study, but their ambition is for them to return and make a good career at home.

Even more significant is the fact that diaspora Jews (including American Jews) have not undergone the experience as an embattled and, at the same time, an occupying power which has led to Israel's willingness to contemplate running risks for peace. It is quite easy to be a hero in Long Island or Golders Green. The whole interlocking character of State-Army relations in Israel and its impact upon the life of every family lies outside their experience.[15] American Jews naturally respond to events pictured for them on their television screens and in the press. They were conscious of the world's disapproval of Israel's Lebabon adventure and there was an upsurge of sentiment for peace seen in the growth of movements like Peace Now. But with the war over, such sentiment subsided.

The new peace process is rooted in the new attitudes of Israelis themselves and assumes the possibility of there being some common fate facing themselves and the Palestinians; they need not only to abstain from military action against each other but to find ways of working together. Most American Jews find this prospect a difficult one to grasp imaginatively and some repudiate it altogether. The most conspicuous of American immigrants in Israel are those who take extreme right-wing positions, often on religious grounds. The massacre in the Mosque at Hebron on 25 February 1994, which was intended to derail the peace process and very nearly did, was perpetrated by an American Jew, and the settlers on the West Bank who glorified in his action owed more to Brooklyn than to Israel.

Such attitudes obviously have no place among the vast majority of American Jews. Hitherto, however, they have not had to face the inevitable dilemma involved in trying to reach a settlement. They could coast along in the comfortable belief that one could have peace and security and retain the territories too. And while Likud was in power in Israel this presented no difficulty. The ambiguities inherent in aspects of the dispute over new boundaries could also be evaded. Opponents of territorial concessions both inside Israel and outside have clung to Begin's "Basic Law on Jerusalem" of 1980, declaring that Jerusalem "whole and united" should be Israel's permanent capital, ignoring the fact that what was now styled Jerusalem was the result of the changes brought about by the 1967 War and did not correspond to the historic Jerusalem of the Zionist dream. Since Jerusalem also had emotional as well as practical significance for the Palestinians, the Jerusalem question could be used as a form of rejecting any settlement. [16]

It was the consciousness of the change of mood within Israel, so it has been argued, that encouraged President Bush to withhold the loan guarantee from the Shamir government, thus branding it as an obstacle to peace, and helping to bring about Rabin's victory in the 1992 election. [17] The advent of Rabin's government made it easier for the peaceably inclined elements in American Jewry to claim that they were once again reflecting the views of Israel's own government. But this did not prevent the development of a vocal opposition to the way the peace process was going or its rejection of the White House Declaration of Principles (DOP) of 13 September 1993. [18] But as we know, the decisions were taken elsewhere. No American Jew was consulted by Rabin or Peres during the secret talks in the summer of 1993 that led to the declaration itself. [19]

Canadian Jewry's response to the DOP was divided along the same lines. [20] In spite of the fact that most of the community was of recent origin and had strong orthodox leanings, there was a good deal of support for the peace process. Canadian rabbis publicly dissented from the action of some US rabbis who wished the community to show its displeasure with Israel's signing of the Declaration by refusing to buy Israeli bonds. [21] In November 1993 there was a meeting between Canadian Jews and Canadian Arabs to discuss the future economic development of the West Bank and Gaza. [22]

In Europe, as already noted, the only significant communities numerically were those of France and Britain. In France, internal problems were all important though it was remembered that Mendès-

France, the most important Jew in post-war French politics, had been an early advocate of attempts to reach a peace with the Arabs.[23]

The divisions in the British Jewish community were not dissimilar from those in the United States – though extreme views on both sides were probably less pronounced. A good deal of criticism was voiced when Yasir Arafat visited London in December 1993 and had talks with Jewish leaders.[24] On the other hand, both religious and secular leaders gave voice to their profound wish to see the peace process succeed. The Hebron massacre brought about the rarity of a public statement signed by leaders in both the Jewish and the Muslim communities. British Jews have, of course, been conscious of the profound hostility to Israel on the part of the Muslim community which has been manifested by action against Jewish or Zionist societies in a number of university campuses. On the other hand, both Muslims and Jews are seen as targets by the new racist upsurge which lumps them all as aliens. Joint action against such dangers would be easier if there were a peace settlement in the Middle East. It is not a matter of lobbying the government but of a public contest for hearts and minds.

Finally one must ask how important diaspora opinions are to the Israelis themselves. The public attitude is one of indifference and this is true also of the official attitude. It has been suggested that even the financial contribution of diaspora Jews could now be dispensed with – though the hard-pressed Israeli universities might dissent from this idea. On the political side, one has the impression that Israel's ambassadors increasingly see their relations with the local Jewish community as one of expounding the Israeli government's own position and less than it used to be of seeking the opinions of their interlocutors. Some Israelis believe that some of the indifference is superficial and that, by and large, Israelis still welcome favourable opinions from the rest of the Jewish world, as a contribution to their self-esteem.

Nevertheless, as the demographic changes make their effect, indifference to what the diaspora can do is likely to grow. What matters will be what happens in Israel and the rest will be marginal. If some form of peace ensures security, even the American Jewish lobby will cease to be valued.

Once national movements have secured a territorial base, language becomes a clear factor of demarcation. More people now speak Hebrew than Norwegian or Danish. More people speak Hebrew than spoke English at the time of Shakespeare. The language is a cement at home, but a barrier against the rest of the world including the vast majority of diaspora Jews who do not use Hebrew outside the synagogue and not always there.

At the same time the pull of geography is making itself felt. Israel is bound to find more and more reasons to eradicate the isolation in which it has lived since its creation. There are already signs that the economic boycott is being diluted and that Israelis will increasingly share with their neighbours the task of tackling the material problems of the Middle East, however slow the progress of the "multilateral" aspects of the peace process.[25] At the level of individuals the interpretation of the two worlds is already beginning. Among the students at the "Desert Research Centre" of the Ben-Gurion University can be found Kuwaitis and Saudis. Can such a process be reversed?

Unlike the United States to which the term was first applied, Israel is indeed a melting pot since every element in the diaspora has contributed to its make-up while the resultant admixture is unlike any of them. Its further evolution will increasingly depend on itself and the value to it of the diaspora will continue to diminish.

NOTES

1. For an account of the situation up to 1988 from a Palestinian perspective see David McDowall, *Palestine and Israel: The Uprising and Beyond*, London, I.B. Tauris, 1989.
2. David Feldman, *Englishmen and Jews: Social Relations and Political Culture 1840–1914*, New Haven and London, Yale University Press, 1994.
3. See for this subject and an analysis of the development of right-wing attitudes in Israel towards Arabs in the 1980s and of the fallacious hopes placed upon the war in Lebanon, Yehoshafat Harkabi, *Israel's Fateful Decisions*, London, I.B. Tauris, 1988.
4. See Avi Shlaim, *Collusion Across the Jordan*, Oxford, Oxford University Press, 1988, or the abridged edition entitled *The Politics of Partition*, Oxford University Press, 1990.
5. George W. Ball and Douglas B. Ball, *The Passionate Attachment: American Involvement with Israel, 1947 to the Present*, New York, Norton, 1992, gives voice to the anti-Israel case.
6. *Economist*, 29 Jan. 1994.
7. For the perspective of Israel's leading historian of Zionism with a close acquaintance with the United States, see David Vital, *The Future of the Jews*, Cambridge, MA, Harvard University Press, 1990.
8. Jonathan Sacks, "From Integration to Survival to Continuity", in Jonathan Webber (ed.), *Jewish Identities in the New Europe*, London and Washington, DC, Littman Library of Jewish Civilization, 1994, p.110.
9. Eliezer Schweid, "Jewish Identities in the New Europe and the Consequences for Israel", in Webber (ed.), *Jewish Identities in the New Europe*, p.45.
10. Ibid., p.44.
11. *Economist*, 29 Jan. 1994.
12. See, for example, Max Beloff, "Lucien Wolf and the Anglo-Russian Entente, 1907–1914", in Max Beloff, *The Intellectual in Politics*, London, Weidenfeld & Nicolson, 1970.
13. See Isaiah Friedman, *The Question of Palestine*, London, Routledge & Kegan Paul, 1973, and his *Germany, Turkey and Zionism 1897–1918*, Oxford, Clarendon Press, 1977.
14. This does not mean that all prominent Democrats are supporters of Israel. Strobe Talbott who holds a high place in the Clinton administration has a long record of public hostility to Israel. See Angelo Codevilla, "Birds of a Feather", *The National Interest*, Spring 1994.
15. For an examination of this problem see Yehuda Ben-Meir, "Civil Military Relations in Israel", in Keith Kyle and Joel Peters (eds.), *Whither Israel: The Domestic Challenges*, London, I.B. Tauris, 1994.
16. See Ian S. Lustick, "Reinventing Jerusalem", *Foreign Policy*, No.93 (Winter 1993–94).
17. See the special supplement, "Les Juifs et la Paix" in the organ of the Belgian Jewish community, *Regards* (Winter 1993–94), pp.10–11.
18. See, for example, David Bar Ilan, "Why a Palestinian State is Still a Mortal Danger", *Commentary*, Nov. 1993, and the correspondence both for and against his argument in

Commentary, Feb. 1994.
19. For an account of these talks by one of the main Israeli intermediaries see the article by Dr Yair Hirschfeld in *Focus* (Autumn 1993), a publication of the University of Haifa.
20. *Globe and Mail* (Toronto), 13 Sept. 1993.
21. *Toronto Star*, 15 Nov. 1993.
22. *Canadian Jewish News*, 3 Feb. 1994.
23. Supplement to *Regards*, pp.6–7.
24. See, for example, *Jewish Chronicle*, 10 Dec. 1993.
25. Extract from remarks by Shimron Peres before the economic committee of the Knesset, *Bipac briefing*, 23 March 1994.

The Boundaries of Peace

MOSHE BRAWER

AMONG THE most difficult if not the most intractable problems which the Arab–Israeli peace process is faced is the delimitation of the boundaries of peace: the borders which in the words of the famous Security Council Resolution 242 will provide Israel with "secure and recognized boundaries free from the threats or acts of force", that is, Israel's boundaries with Lebanon, Syria, Jordan and what will most probably become a Palestinian state; the boundary with Egypt is fully accepted and demarcated, by both sides, under the Egyptian–Israeli peace treaty.

The complexity of the subject is not only due to the political and military developments since the establishment of the State of Israel (1948), but is deeply affected by the widespread transformation in the nature and pattern of the urban and rural population which has taken place over the last seven decades. The present size, distribution and composition of the population over most of the country is fundamentally different from that at the early stages of the conflict. On top of this come the long and rich historic aspescts and religious sentiments, inherent in the Holy Land, which cannot be avoided whenever issues concerning the political future of the country are raised. Another source of difficulties and complications are the physical attributes of the country and its poverty in natural resources (especially water) which do not lend themselves easily to division and to boundary-making.

The Holy Land was the first country in human history to have accurately delimited boundaries (Old Testament, Numbers 34/3–12). These boundaries had undergone numerous changes during biblical and post-biblical times, and there is wide divergence of opinion among scholars and rabbinical authorities as to the extent of the areas which should be considered as the "Holy Land". It should also be remembered that the country regained its status as a separate political entity, as British–administered Palestine, only after the First World War. Before that, for over 600 years (since the collapse of the state of the Crusaders) it

Moshe Brawer is Professor of Geography at Tel-Aviv University. This analysis is based largely on research and fieldwork carried out by members of the academic staff and graduate students of the Department of Geography at Tel-Aviv University.

only consisted of several administrative units in other Middle East states.

The present boundaries of Israel, according to their origin, belong to two categories: boundaries created by colonial powers during the first quarter of the twentieth century, and boundaries which came into being since the birth of Israel, formally "armistice lines", "cease fire lines", or "lines of separation". Some of these are known locally as the "Green Line", the colour in which they were first overprinted on official Israeli maps.

COLONIAL BOUNDARIES

Britain played a dominant role in the delimitation of colonial boundaries. The Egyptian–Israeli boundary, which had originally come into being in 1906 as the boundary between the British and Ottoman Empires, was actually imposed by Britain on the Turks to give Britain full control of the Sinai Peninsula. It was fully demarcated and institutionalized in a delimitation agreement.[1] It remained unchanged during British rule in Palestine (1918–48) despite much pressure in the early 1920s to draw a new boundary between both countries.[2] At the time this 210 km-long boundary was created, there were no sedentary inhabitants in the desert region which it crosses, except for a small hamlet, Rafah, near its northern end close to the Mediterranean coast. Several bedouin tribes roamed mainly the northern part of this newly-imposed frontier zone. Their movements and grazing and water resources were not immediately affected by this boundary.

Under the 1979 Egyptian–Israeli peace treaty, followed by international arbitration to settle differences concerning the position of small segments of the boundary, the 1906 boundary was fully restored and newly demarcated. It now forms the only peace boundary which Israel has. The areas close to the northern (Mediterranean) and the southern (Gulf of Aqaba) ends of this boundary are densely inhabited by urban populations. The status and functions of the northern-most section (about ten kilometres) of this boundary, separating the Gaza Strip from Egyptian Sinai, were subject to serious difficulties during the Israeli–Palestinian negotiations which preceded the agreement under which Israel evacuated the Gaza Strip. Under this agreement Israel continues to maintain full control of this section so that the autonomous Gaza Strip has no territorial contact with neighbouring Egypt. This, however, is likely to undergo some changes in the future, when the Gaza Strip will become part of a Palestinian entity.

The Palestine–Transjordan Boundary

The second phase in colonial boundary making came in 1922 when the British government decided to separate Transjordan (now Jordan) from Palestine, both of which were at the time administered by Britain under a League of Nations mandate. The Order in Council which announced this step was accompanied by an Order by the High Commissioner for Palestine and Transjordan which delimited the boundary between these two territories as "a line drawn from a point two miles west of Aqaba up the centre of Wadi Araba, the Dead Sea and the river Jordan to the junction of the latter with the river Yarmuk, thence up the centre of the river Yarmuk to the Syrian frontier."[3] At the time this was effectively an internal administrative boundary between two British-administered territories crossing almost uninhabited areas. Except for four kilometres in the extreme south, from the shores of the Gulf of Aqaba, demarcated in 1946, this boundary remained only vaguely marked on maps. Shortly after the publication of the Order concerning the establishment of this boundary, it was decided in the offices of the British administration in Jerusalem that in so far as the Wadi Araba (that is, the Valley of Araba or Arava, the rift valley between the Dead Sea and the Gulf of Aqaba) was concerned, the "centre of the valley" of the above mentioned Order should imply the "line of lowest points". This interpretation, which had no legal authorization, was applied when the boundary was first marked on maps available then (1923). These maps were not based on an authentic survey of the Wadi Araba and were grossly inaccurate so that the boundary drawn on them did not concur even with the actual "line of lowest points". Nevertheless, it was copied into all maps published from then on by the British administration of both Palestine and Trans-jordan as well as by other map-makers. Repeated requests by the director of the Survey Department to clarify the exact position of this boundary throughout the Wadi Araba, and to demarcate it were rejected by the competent British authorities.[4] This boundary, as inaccurately inserted into official maps, became the Israeli–Jordanian armistice line in 1949. The exact position of this boundary, as decreed by the former British authorities, is not clear to the present day, except, as mentioned, the southern-most four kilometres that were demarcated when Transjordan (now Jordan) gained its independence. The necessity to review the existing delimitation and to demarcate the boundary in the Wadi Araba has already been raised in the recent Israeli–Jordanian peace negotiations. All water courses in the Wadi Araba are dry throughout the year except for a few days during winter, when they carry sporadic gushes of water. The channels through which these short flash floods flow shift frequently.

The Dead Sea

Across the Dead Sea the boundary followed closely a line equidistant from its eastern and western shores. Here again it was only marked on maps, not even the entrance point of the boundary (in the south) and its exit (in the north) were demarcated. However, in the early 1920s the level of the Dead Sea was comparatively high – 390 metres (or even 389 metres) below the level of the Mediterranean. At that time it expanded over low-lying areas along its shores, especially along the southern shores where it is bordered by flat swampy areas, and was still untouched by human intervention. The sea level has since fallen by nearly 14 metres, which caused it to shrink considerably. Its shallow southern basin had dried up and was turned into a series of artificial salt pans operated by the Israeli and Jordanian Potash companies, respectively. The continuous fall in the level of the sea is the result of the diversion of the waters of the Jordan (which drains into the Dead Sea and has been its main water source) and its main tributaries into the supply systems of Israel and of Jordan. The fact that the western part of the main basin of the sea is comparatively much shallower than the deep eastern part caused the median line to move considerably eastward, following the extreme fall in the level of the sea. Thus the boundary across what remains today of the sea has shifted eastward, towards the Jordanian coast, when compared with its position when first delimited in 1922. Further, the narrow part of the sea, opposite the Lissan Peninsula, has dried up completely so that a new land contact between Israel and Jordan has been formed along several kilometres, requiring the delimitation and demarcation of a new boundary.

Under the completely new physical conditions which now prevail over much of what has been the Dead Sea in its natural form, the Israeli–Jordanian peace talks will have to solve a number of problems and agree on a new dividing line across the sea. A tacit understanding on the limits of each side in the utilization of the resources of the sea has actually been in existence for a good many years.

The Boundary Along the Rivers Jordan and Yamuk

The course of the river Jordan, from its junction with the river Yarmuk to the Dead Sea, in what is known as the Lower Jordan Valley, meanders extensively through a one-to-two-kilometre-wide flood plain. The distance between the Yarmuk junction and the Dead Sea is approximately 85 kilometres, while the length of the course of the Jordan between these points is nearly 200 kilometres. As long as the river carried its full natural flow its channel shifted frequently, abandoning "old" meanders and forming new ones. Occasionally the stream bifurcated, creating small islands, but these were not permanent features, at least in so far as location and extent were concerned. Thus, here, too, the exact position of the boundary was unclear. Taking literally the wording of the official Order of Delimitation, the boundary must have shifted slightly frequently over numerous sections of the river channel. Hardly any attention had been paid to these changes, since the banks of the river Jordan and adjoining areas throughout most of the Lower Jordan Valley were almost uninhabited. It is only in the northern part of this valley, close to the junction with the river Yarmuk and opposite the Beisan Valley that there were villages and cultivated land which reached the vicinity of the banks of the Jordan. The more significant shifts in the channel of the Jordan in this part of the valley affected the lands of some of these villages. In one such case (1927) the change in the course of the river, following floods, resulted in the transfer of several hundred acres from the western to the eastern side of the Jordan. The British administration ruled then that the boundary should shift with the course of the river. As a result mandatory Palestine lost some lands to Transjordan.[5]

The greatly reduced discharge of the river Jordan since the 1960s, with the diversion of most of its flow by Israel and of that of its main tributary, the Yarmuk, by the Kingdom of Jordan, has diminished considerably, almost eliminated, most of the features of the above-mentioned natural behaviour. There were hardly any changes in the course of the river in recent years. On the other hand, because of the low water level, even during the height of winter, there are many more permanent small islands, some of which may be utilized for agricultural purposes. Another conspicuous change is the large increase of population and in cultivated lands extending to the vicinity of the river, which has taken place (especially on the Jordanian side) since the 1960s, along much of the Lower Jordan Valley. The determination of the exact position of the boundary along the river Jordan, perhaps accompanied by demarcation where possible, is on the agenda of the peace talks between both countries.

The river Yarmuk along which the Palestinian–Transjordan boundary ran for about 18 kilometres flows through most of its course in a deep narrow gorge. Only at its lower part, where it approaches its confluence with the river Jordan, does it enter the flat open country of the Lower Jordan Valley. In this part frequent changes in the course of the channel have taken place, in particular after large flash floods. As in the case of Jordan, this resulted in local shifts in the location of the boundary. These movements in the boundary line were in some cases not accepted by the farming communities whose lands bordered on the banks of the Yarmuk. Although only very small areas were involved, they continued to hold and cultivate their lands (whenever possible) even after these changed sides in so far as the flow of the river was concerned. Under a concession granted in the early 1920s by the British authorities in both Palestine and Transjordan, an Israeli company (the Palestine Electric Co.) built a hydro-electric power station utilizing the junction of the Jordan and the Yarmuk. For this purpose the course of the Yarmuk was diverted southward to shorten its way to the Jordan. The power station, which stood on Transjordanian territory, was dismantled in 1948, but the actual boundary (armistice line) followed the shortened diverted course of the Yarmuk. The Jordanian government now claims the area (a few hundred acres), held by Israel, between the old natural junction of the rivers and that of its present position.

It should be noted that if the present agreed process of turning the West Bank into an autonomous region would lead to the establishment of a Palestinian state, a substantial part of the above discussed boundary along the Dead Sea and the river Jordan would turn into a boundary between the latter state and Jordan.

The British–French Boundary

The third and last part of the colonial boundaries, that with Lebanon and Syria, received its final shape in 1923, following lengthy negotiations between Britain and France. Lebanon and Syria came after the First World War under French control as a League of Nations mandated territory, similar to the status of the British administration of Palestine. This boundary was also accurately mapped and demarcated by a mixed Anglo-French military commission.[6] The western part of this boundary, between Mandatory Palestine (now Israel) and Lebanon, begins on the Mediterranean coast at a small cape, Rosh Ha'niqra or Ras al-Naqura, where the highlands of Galilee reach the sea in a long line of high white cliffs. From here eastward it follows mostly local minor physical features in a mountainous terrain moderately populated by numerous small villages. At the time of demarcation much attention was paid to the limits of cultivable lands of the villages in what was to become the frontier zone, so that the new boundary would not cut off villages from their sources of livelihood. In its eastern-most section this part of the boundary makes a sharp turn northward (see Map 1) so as to include in Palestine the entire Hula Valley (the northern-most part of the Jordan Rift Valley) and the highlands overlooking it on its western side. The boundary was also so drawn here as to include in Mandatory Palestine the only three Jewish settlements at that time (1923) in this part of the country. In 1937 the British administration constructed a barbed wire wall with police towers to prevent the infiltration of armed hostile elements from Lebanon. This was thus for several years the first part of the boundaries of Palestine to become a closed barrier.

Statements of policy made recently by Israel and Lebanon make it clear that both sides fully accept this boundary. It may be necessary to make some local minor rectifications in the boundary line so as to improve its functions and to facilitate its protection against unlawful activities. This would involve small exchanges of territory. Israel controls at present a several kilometres-wide strip of Lebanese territory

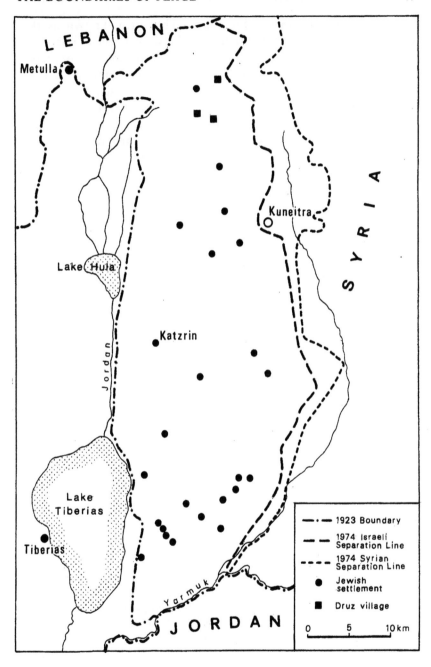

along the above-mentioned boundary. This strip, known as the "security zone", is in fact a buffer zone between Israel and areas in Southern Lebanon actually controlled by local militant organizations. The internal conditions which prevailed in Lebanon during and after its long civil war, when "private armies" and various armed militias gained control over large parts of the country, prompted Israel to extend its control to the mentioned strip north of its boundary with Lebanon. Some of the Lebanese organizations persist in armed attacks against targets in northern Israel. It is assumed that once the Lebanese government is in a position effectively to enforce law and order in the frontier zone adjoining Israel, there would be no need for this security zone.

The Upper Jordan Valley and Its Lakes

The main characteristics of the eastern parts of this British–French boundary, namely that between Mandatory Palestine (now Israel) and Syria, is the conspicuous British endeavour to have full control of the waters of the river Jordan, including the two lakes: Hula and Tiberias through which the river flows. The groups of springs, Dan and Banias, which feed the main head streams of the Jordan, were allocated to Palestine. Beyond these springs the boundary turned southward and was drawn almost parallel to the course of the Jordan, but a short distance (not more than 200 metres) east of its eastern bank. The same applies to the mentioned lakes. Along the north-eastern coast of Lake Tiberias the boundary was placed only ten metres away from the shore line. Syrian villages living close to the coast of Lake Tiberias were permitted to draw water from the lake but had to obtain annual permits from the British authorities in Tiberias to fish in the lake.[7] The boundary gave Mandatory Palestine full control of both banks of the Jordan, throughout the Upper Jordan Valley, as well as of the entire area and coasts of Lake Hula (almost completely drained by Israel in the 1950s) and Lake Tiberias. On the other hand, the high escarpment rising from the eastern fringes of the Upper Jordan Valley to the Golan plateau, generally known as the Golan Heights, was left almost entirely to the French (Syria). Only opposite the southern part of Lake Tiberias, approaching the Yarmuk gorge, does the boundary rise from the bottom of the escarpment to the vicinity of its upper part.

On reaching the narrow deep valley of the Yarmuk this boundary made a sharp turn eastward and for four kilometres followed the precipitous northern slopes of this valley to a point on the Yarmuk where the boundaries of Mandatory Palestine (Israel), Syria and Trans-jordan (Jordan) meet. This gave Mandatory Palestine a narrow strip of territory, 300 metres to one kilometre wide, which protruded eastward from the Jordan valley along the banks of the Yarmuk river. This territory is known as the "Hamma Strip", Hammat Geder or Hamma, being a small spa at the eastern end of this strip. The southern side of this part of the Yarmuk valley along the Hamma Strip was included in Transjordan, then also under British rule, so that the entire lower part of the Yarmuk valley came under British control. This seemed at the time of the delimitation of this boundary an important gain in view of plans to build a railway through the Yarmuk valley from Haifa to Baghdad (which never materialized), and to lay pipelines from Iraqi oilfields to the Mediterranean coast.[8] This narrow protrusion of Mandatory Palestinian (later Israeli) territory along the lower Yarmuk was the source of numerous violent incidents between Israel and Syria in the early 1950s. Israel was forced to withdraw from this strip and only regained it in 1967.

After the final signing of the Anglo-French delimitation and demarcation agreement came a French request to rectify the boundary in the extreme north-east, near the Banias springs (an important source of one of the head streams of the Jordan). The French required a small area which would include the Banias springs for a vital road to connect south-western Syria with the ports of southern Lebanon. They were allowed to take temporary control of the requested territory (about two square kilometres), and the matter was referred for final settlement to the British and French governments. The issue remained "open", with the French actually holding the area by the time the French left Syria (1945) and the British Palestine (1948).[9] This small but vital area in so far as water resources were concerned was taken over by Syria after the French departed and was likely to figure prominently in future boundary negotiations between Israel and Syria.

POST-1948 BOUNDARIES

The birth of Israel, the Palestine War (1948–49), the Six Day War (1967) and the Yom Kippur War (1973) resulted in the appearance of new boundaries in addition to those parts of the former colonial boundaries which remained in force. All these new boundaries have the official status of armistice lines, cease fire lines, or separation lines, and are therefore, at least formally, temporary. Some had undergone changes in status following war operations. Thus the 1949 armistice line between Israel and Jordan became a cease fire line after the 1967 War, even where its position remained unchanged. The same armistice line along the West Bank, which had been to all practical purposes an international boundary (1949–67), became an internal administrative boundary within the areas controlled by Israel after the Six Day War. There are also small segments where a de facto boundary came into being not on the basis of any of the above-mentioned formal types. All these new boundaries are long stretches demarcated by defensive fences. Their exact position is also mapped in detail, even where they have changed from closed international barriers to open internal administrative divisions. The delimitation of these new "temporary" boundaries left small areas of "no man's land", where no agreed line could be drawn between the positions each side held when fighting stopped.

The Gaza Strip

The first of the new boundaries to be based on a formal internationally recognized agreement was the Israel–Egyptian armistice line signed in early 1949, which actually created the Gaza Strip, a bulge of Egyptian-held territory along the southern coast of British Palestine with Gaza as its urban centre (see Map 2). The extent of the Gaza Strip, as delimited and later demarcated, followed to a large extent the front line at the time a cease fire came into force in January 1949. Mutual small local concessions were made by each side to adapt the boundary to some local factors. In the south Israel withdrew from a two-to-three-kilometre-wide strip in the neighbourhood of the main road connecting Gaza with Egypt, to give the Egyptian army better control of this road. In the north the Egyptians gave up a similar area to enable Israel to take full possession of a small seasonal stream (Nahal Shiqma), later used to enhance the water resources of the neighbourhood. It so happened that this boundary followed approximately the eastern limit of the sedentary Arab population of the southern part of the Palestinian coastal plain and of their permanently cultivated lands. The sedentary populations east of this new boundary consisted mainly of a few small Jewish settlements established in the 1940s. There was also, east of the boundary, a semi-nomad and a nomad Arab population which moved into the Gaza Strip during spells of fighting which preceded the armistice agreement.[10]

Immediately after its imposition by the armistice agreement the boundary became also a distinct line of ethnic division, whereby all inhabitants within the Gaza Strip were Arabs while the population around its external perimeter was purely Jewish. Except for the Gaza Strip, the Egyptian–Israeli 1949 armistice line concurred with the 1906 colonial boundary down to the coast of the Gulf of Aqaba.

Prior to the outbreak of the Palestine War (1948), the population of the Gaza Strip stood at about 80,000, nearly half of whom resided in the urban area of Gaza. The population subsisted mainly on agriculture and most of the strip was sparsely populated. The population more than trebled as a result of the influx during 1948–49 of a large number of refugees from areas which came under Israeli control. A high birth rate and natural increase has since brought the population to its present level of more than 700,000, making the Gaza Strip one of the most densely

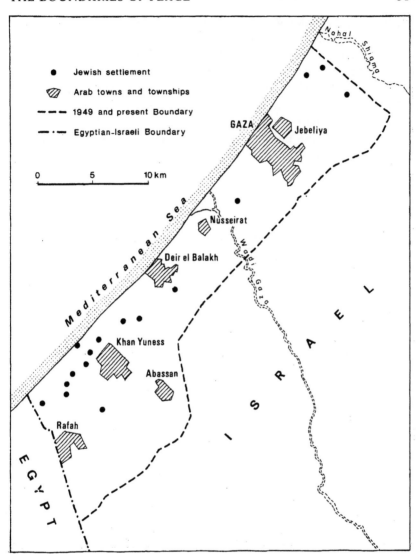

inhabited areas in the Middle East. Local resources (agricultural land and water) are scanty and fully exploited, providing subsistence only for a small part of the population. The great majority depend on outside work and on aid. After the strip came under Israelil control in 1967, a growing number of its inhabitants were allowed to seek employment in Israel. Unemployment was substantially reduced and the economic plight of a large part of the population was considerably eased. At its height in 1988, the number of Gaza Strip inhabitants who found employment in Israel exceeded 50,000, or nearly 50 per cent of the male labour force. This source of livelihood has shrunk considerably in recent years as a result of the *intifada* and acts of violence carried out in Israel by Gaza Strip inhabitants. The boundaries of the Gaza Strip under the 1993 autonomy agreement are almost identical with the 1949 armistice line. There are only minor local divergencies resulting from the new road system built along the eastern margin of the strip to avoid its densely inhabited interior. There are two exceptions in so far as the extent of the Gaza Strip territory is concerned: the enclaves of Israeli settlements established over the last 20 years inside the strip; and a narrow Israeli buffer zone, along the Egyptian boundary, in the south, separating the autonomous Gaza Strip from Egypt (see Map 2).

There are 14 Jewish settlements, with a population of nearly 5,000, inside the strip, controlling approximately five per cent of its territory. The settlers engage mainly in highly advanced, scientifically and techni-cally, agriculture, producing vegetables and flowers (mainly for export) on dunes previously considered uncultivable. Under the autonomy agreement these settlements remain under full Israeli control as enclaves connected by special roads to neighbouring Israeli territory. It is likely that several of the smaller and more isolated of these settlements would be abandoned some time after the autonomy agreement is fully imple-mented. The rest of the settlements would most probably be given up following the next stage in the peace process between Israel and the Palestinians when the autonomy would be replaced by more permanent arrangements.

The West Bank

The armistice agreement between Israel and Jordan, signed in the spring of 1949, delimited a boundary which was made up partly by the former colonial boundary between Mandatory Palestine and Trans-jordan, but also produced a completely new boundary across the central highlands of Palestine, the historical regions of Judea and Samaria. This latter boundary, though based to a great extent on the position of the front lines when a UN-initiated and supervised cease fire came into force, was actually superimposed on densely inhabited rural and urban areas. The determination of the exact location of this sensitive new line was left almost entirely to senior army officers on both sides and on behalf of the UN, who had no previous experience in drawing such lines. It was also assumed at the time that the armistice agreement would be followed within a few months by peace talks that would lead to a more enduring settlement and to the creation of a more carefully delimited boundary. Talks under UN auspices actually started in Lausanne later the same summer but they soon ended in complete deadlock.

Two main considerations were actually responsible for the shaping of the new boundary which enclosed on the north, west and south, what came to be known as the West Bank (at that time of the Kingdom of Jordan): military (or strategic) factors, and important arteries of communication. Hardly any attention was paid to the effects which the new boundary, a practically sealed barrier, would have on the population of the newly-created frontier zone. The military factors which dominated mutual perceptions as to what would be a good armistice line were based largely on the types of weapons and other military equipment available to each side in those days. Most of these considerations became obsolete within a decade. In so far as arteries of communication were concerned, Israel insisted on the surrender of territory which would enable it to restore vital railway and road links, severed during the war. These included the railway and main road to Jerusalem (the western part of which became Israel's capital), the railway and main road along the eastern fringes of the coastal plain connecting Tel-Aviv with Haifa (Israel's primary port at the time), and the main road from the coastal plain to the Galilee (the Nahal Eron or Wadi Ara road). Some of these communication lines passed through "no man's land" between the military positions of both sides, others crossed territory held by the Jordanians short distances east of the front line. The Jordanians met some of these Israeli requests; this entailed their withdrawal from small areas in densely inhabited rural part of western Samaria which included several large Arab villages ceded to Israel. The main road between Tel-Aviv and Jerusalem remained closed as the Jordanians would not relent in their objections to the use of a strip of "no man's land" for the reopening of a vital section of this road. This also prevented the resumption of the modern water supply to Jerusalem from the coastal plain (installed by the British administration). In return for territory ceded by Jordan, Israel retreated from a small area in the south-western corner of the West Bank.

The new boundary of the West Bank, generally known in Israel as "the Green Line", had many faults and oversights even for a temporary short-lived barrier, which in turn resulted in numerous violent border incidents. The line cut across villages, leaving one part of each of these villages on the Israeli side of the boundary, and the other on the

Jordanian side. Some villages were cut off from a substantial, if not most, of their water resources. Shortly after the imposition of this boundary it became impassable by effective barbed wire fences or even minefields. The new boundary also cut across the agricultural lands of many villages, some of which lost most of their cultivable lands. In most cases, villages located on the western foothills of Samaria were left on the Jordanian side of the boundary, while much of their culti-vated lands and other main sources of livelihood remained on the Israeli side and became inaccessible to their inhabitants (see Map 3). Most of the Arab villages on the western foothills of the central highlands were dependent prior to 1948 not only on agricultural lands but also, to a great extent, on employment and vital services in the coastal plain. Thus the new boundary made many of the inhabitants of these villages destitute. Between 1950 and 1967 many of these villagers, especially young males, emigrated to other Arab countries.[11]

Some of the evils of this boundary were at least partly rectified during the demarcation process which took several years to complete when small local exchanges of territory or deviations from the original delimitation agreement were made. In this way several villages regained access to their water resources or to some orchards and plantations, but these were only minute improvements. On the other hand, Israel was unable fully to utilize important arteries of communication, which were now formally under its control. The new boundary did not provide sufficient space for the safe and efficient operation of transport systems. A section of the railway to Jerusalem passed within a few steps of the boundary. The same applied to the railway and road along the eastern fringes of the coastal plain. Incidents and tensions along these sections considerably limited the use of the railways and road. The shortcomings of the armistice agreement in so far as the network of main communication lines was concerned had to be overcome on both sides by the construction of new road and railway links to replace those the use of which was denied as a result of the war.

The urban area of Jerusalem was subject to a number of special arrangements within the armistice agreement. The delimitation of the boundary across the heart of the city which divided it into two almost completely isolated parts was fully based on the positions each side held when the fighting stopped. An agreement between the local military commanders which preceded the armistice agreement by several months paved the way for the division of the city. A narrow strip of "no man's land" separated the respective boundaries of each side. Here again the boundary inside the city had a distinct military flavour, hardly leaving any room for other considerations. The boundary also had a conspicuous ethno-religious character. The population of the Israeli (western) part of the city became almost entirely Jewish (the

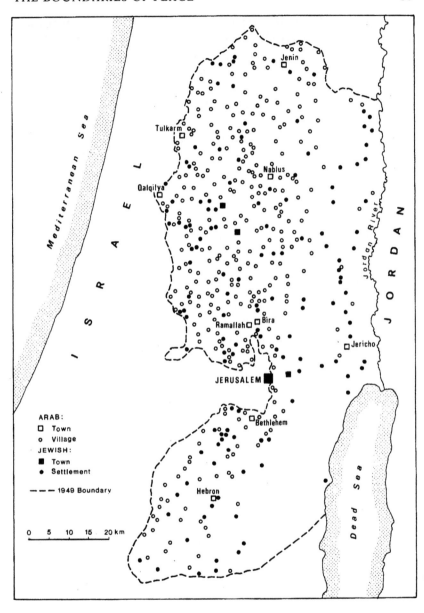

ARAB:
□ Town
o Village
JEWISH:
■ Town
● Settlement
— — — 1949 Boundary

0 5 10 15 20 km

Arab inhabitants fled to the eastern part), while the Jordanian part was Arab, with samll non-Arab Christian communities. Each part of the city developed its own independent water and electricity supply and other vital services. The sewage system remained largely unaffected by the boundary. The ethnic division of the 1949 boundary across the city has not been maintained since 1967, when eastern Jerusalem was annexed by Israel. Large numbers of Jews settled in what had been eastern (Jordanian) Jerusalem and its surroundings.[12]

The conversion in the summer of 1967 of the boundary between Israel and the West Bank from a closed international barrier to an open internal administrative border has had far-reaching effects on both Israel and the West Bank. Israel's coastal plain, with its dense urban, industrial and agricultural population, became accessible to the Arab inhabitants of Palestine's central highlands, especially to the rural and urban population of its western fringes. The villages in the former Jordanian frontier zone, which became destitute in 1949, were the first to enjoy the economic benefits of the new situation. Their lands on the Israeli side of the border were not restored to them, but they found ample, comparatively highly-paid employment in Israel. Gradually a mutual dependence developed between a growing part of the West Bank labour force and the rapidly expanding Israeli economy and labour market. The dependence on work in Israel is especially strong in many villages in areas of the West Bank adjoining Israel. The lands at the disposal of these villages are poor, with highly fragmented owner-ship. They can provide subsistence only to a small part of their inhabi-tants who have more than doubled in number since 1967. These lands, due to their geological and pedological characteristics, do not lend themselves to intensive agricultural development. On the other hand, the neighbouring areas of Israel have at the moment and in the fore-seeable future no better source of manual labour for their agricultural, industrial and building expanding activities. Short periods in recent years during which a closure was imposed on the West Bank have clearly proved this reality.

Another crucial development that followed the above-mentioned conversion in the status and functions of West Bank boundaries has been the establishment of numerous Jewish settlements all over the West Bank. Most of these settlements are small, both in terms of population and in the amount of land they occupy, but there are a number of larger villages and several townships, some of which are in fact suburban residential outposts of neighbouring towns in Israel. This is particularly true of the many settlements in West Bank areas adjacent to Israel. There are at present 128 such settlements with a total population of approximately 110,000 (nearly 12 per cent of the popula-tion in the West Bank). With the exception of Hebron, where Jewish settlement activities have taken place inside an Arab town, the sites of all other settlements were previously uninhabited. In a number of cases, Jewish settlements abandoned in 1948 in areas occupied by Jordan were re-established after the Israeli occupation of the West Bank. Only a small number of these Jewish settlements (mostly in the Lower Jordan Valley) engage in agriculture. Most of the lands which they use have not been cultivated before. Modern agricultural techniques and irrigation made the exploitation of these lands possible. Modern industries have been established in some of the settlements, mainly in the townships. They provide employment for a small percentage of the settlers, in some cases for Arab villagers from the neighbourhood as well. The great majority of the Jewish settlers in the West Bank, however, depend on employment in Israel, on Israeli government-financed activities or on funds provided by political and social Jewish organizations. Many settlers have moved to the West Bank because of the very favourable conditions under which housing could be acquired. Housing projects for Jewish settlers in the West Bank were very heavily subsidized in the 1980s by the then ruling Likud government. The future of these settlements is one of the main problems with which Israeli-Palestinian negotiators would be faced.

THE WEST BANK WATER PROBLEM

Another issue with which the future boundaries of the West Bank are tied up is that of water resources. Groundwater resources provide most of the water requirements on the densely inhabited Israeli coastal plain. A substantial part, if not most, of these resources originate in rains which fall during the winter months over the western slopes of the highlands of the West Bank. The rock formations of these highlands are highly pervious so that most of the rain seeps deep into the ground and flows deep underground westward towards the coastal plain. Some of these underground flows appear in Israeli territory in the form of large springs which used to feed the few perennial rivers of the coastal plain. These springs and many hundreds of wells, all strictly controlled by an Israeli national water authority, tap to the utmost the available groundwater resources to meet the requirements of the Israeli population and its economic activities. The water supply to consumers in Israel is rationed, by quotas to agriculture and industry and by high prices (when reasonable consumption is exceeded) to households. In recent years Israel has barely met its water requirements even in years of normal winter rainfall. Supplies had to be cut, especially to agriculture, when rainfall was well below the average annual quantities. Groundwater resources in the coastal plain are also artificially fed by modern techniques, by damming seasonal and sporadic streams and by water brought in pipes from the better provided north-east.

Until quite recently, the groundwater which flows deep underground from the West Bank into the Israeli coastal plain was technically inaccessible to the inhabitants of the West Bank. Only a small amount of these waters was available in the West Bank from numerous small springs and shallow wells. Much of the water supply of the West Bank, especially in villages, came from rain-water collected in cisterns and reservoirs. In recent decades geological research and advanced hydrological techniques have been used to locate and tap deep underground flows. This should enable public and private organizations in the West Bank to draw a substantial amount, if not most, of the groundwater which since immemorial times has reached the coastal plain. Should this happen, it would deprive Israel of one of its main and most vital sources of water. This is likely to have a disastrous effect on Israel's highly developed agriculture and also on the water-bearing rock formations (aquifer) of the coastal plain by upsetting the equilibrium which prevents the seepage of sea water into some of these formations.[13] Since Israel gained control of the West Bank, strict limits were imposed on the boring and utilization of deep wells which could interfere with the normal flow of groundwater towards the coastal plain. Israel is anxious to ensure that the groundwater flows from the western part of the West Bank would not be tampered with to an extent that would be detrimental to its water resources. This can be achieved by the delimitation of a new boundary, five to seven kilometres east of the present western boundary of the West Bank, so that the foothills of Samaria (which, as mentioned, are economically dependent on Israel) would be ceded to Israel. Another possibility is the imposition of an effective control on the development of water resources in the western part of the West Bank to prevent any serious damage to groundwater resources in the coastal plain.

The West Bank is also burdened with serious water problems. The rapidly growing population and the continuous rise in the standard of living have greatly increased the water consumption. The available resources at present are insufficient so that shortages, growing in seriousness, are experienced. The main sources of the West Bank are springs and groundwater of the eastern parts of the central highlands. A large part of the winter rains which fall on the West Bank drain, both as surface run-off and underground, flows towards the Lower Jordan Valley and the Dead Sea. Israel has little access to these resources and actually uses them to a small extent to supply some of the Jewish settlements in the eastern part of the West Bank. These resources which are entirely within the West Bank are not yet fully exploited, however; the potential increase in supply from these sources would ease for a few years the water shortages, but cannot solve the water problems of the region.[14]

JERICHO

The town of Jericho and its surroundings, the first part of the West Bank to which the Israeli–Palestinian autonomy agreement has been applied, is in fact an oasis surrounded by an arid, almost desert-like uninhabited environment. It is situated in the south-western part of the Lower Jordan Valley, about 380 metres below sea level, the lowest town on earth. Believed to be one of the oldest towns in the Middle East, Jericho subsists largely on 5,000 acres of irrigated lands, mostly orchards and market gardening. It has its own rich water supply, provided by springs within the bounds of the town and the conduit from a large spring a few kilometres west of the town. The oasis has been famous since biblical times for its early vegetables and fruit. It is also famous for its archaelogical excavations which include the remains of the ancient biblical town. With a population of approximately 20,000, Jericho is, despite its natural isolation, a market and services centre to a wide area sparsely inhabited by bedouins, but also to several Jewish settlements established in recent years in its neighbourhood (but not included in the autonomous area). The town is also a transit centre for traffic between the West Bank and Jordan. The only road to Allenby Bridge, the main crossing point over the river to Jordan, passes through Jericho. Good roads make it easily accessible to Jerusalem and most parts of the West Bank.

THE GOLAN HEIGHTS

The most recent of the "new" boundaries is that between Israel and Syria on the Golan plateau and the slopes of Mount Hermon (the southern-most part of the Anti-Lebanon range), the region generally known as the Golan Heights (see Map 1). Formally, here are two almost parallel lines of separation, delimited (through US mediation) and demarcated in the spring of 1974. The western line is the actual boundary between Israel and Syria, a sealed and closely guarded line. The eastern line, one to seven kilometres further east, marks the limits of a demilitarized zone under the supervision of a UN international force. The area between these two lines is subject to Syrian civil administration and is inhabited by Syrians. This boundary is the direct result of two periods of war between both countries, during which Israel occupied the area between the former colonial boundary and a line beyond the present "line of separation", and six years later (1973) repulsed a Syrian offensive to retake this area; in 1974 Israel retreated from part of the area it occupied, under an agreement which included the delimitation of the above-mentioned lines of separation. Since then this has been the most peaceful part of Israel's boundaries with its neighbours.

Prior to the Israeli occupation, the Golan Heights had (according to Syrian official sources) a population of approximately 80,000. They lived in nearly 40 villages and hamlets and one township. It was an ethnically and religiously mixed population of Circassians, Druzes, Alawites and Sunni Arabs. Except for four Druze villages in the extreme south, with 6,000 inhabitants, the entire population left the region with the withdrawal of the Syrian army. Agriculture and stock raising were the main occupations of the former Syrian inhabitants. The Druze population which remained in the Israeli-held Golan has more than doubled since. Many of them are employed in Israel.[15]

The main original motive behind the Israeli offensive which led to the occupation of the Golan in 1967 had been the security of the Jewish settlements in the Hula Valley, the Upper Jordan Valley and the surroundings of Lake Tiberias. Syrian attacks from the overlooking dominating heights of the Golan escarpment caused much damage and constant anxiety in many of these settlements. These attacks came mainly during numerous violent border incidents along the armistice line in the 1950s and 1960s, connected with Israeli development projects (draining Lake Hula, diversion of water from the river Jordan) to which the Syrians objected. There were also many disputes concerning agricultural lands in the frontier zone. The Syrians, for their part, began to build a canal along the western escarpment of the Golan in order to divert one of the head streams of the river Jordan and deprive Israel of its waters. Israel tried to obstruct the progress of this work. The geographical advantages which the upper part of the Golan escarpment gave the Syrians often put Israel militarily in conspicuous inferiority. Hence the desire to dislodge the Syrians from their dominating positions. In fact the Israeli army advanced well beyond the western fringes of the Golan, occupied much of the region, and got within sight of Damascus.

Thirty-two Israeli settlements, including one township (Katzrin), with a total population of over 12,000, have since been established on the Golan plateau, most of them in the 1970s. Modern industries were also attracted to this region. It became Israel's most prestigious wine-producing area. Modern and highly sophisticated agriculture and dairying made many of these new settlements prosperous. The region has become highly developed, equipped with an efficient modern infrastructure and vital services most of which it never had before. It has become a model of a highly advanced social and economic rural community. However, with a population of less than 30,000 (including the Druze villages in the north), the Israeli-held part of the Golan is only sparsely inhabited. The Syrian part of the Golan, east of the boundary, though much inferior in its development, is more densely populated. In 1981 Israel actually annexed the area it holds on the Golan Heights.[16]

It is widely agreed among Israeli military experts that the Golan has lost since 1967 much, if not most, of its military importance to Israel. There are differences of opinion as to what role parts of the Golan may play in the future in the defence of Israel, especially if proper security arrangements are made under a peace treaty with Syria.[17] In addition to the historic and sentimental attachment to the Golan by a great number of the Jewish population of Israel, there is the crucial problem of the control of its water resources. Israel now controls all the small tributaries which drain the Golan directly into the Jordan Valley as well as a large tributary of the Yarmuk (which itself is a tributary of the Jordan). The Golan is well endowed with precipitation and is an important catchment area for substantial quantities of water which find their way into the Jordan, namely, into Israel's water supply system. There is hardly any doubt that once Israel gives up its control of the Golan, especially of its western fringes, Syria, which has projects to develop its south-western region, would divert most of the waters of the Golan for its own use. The final position of the boundary in this region would most probably be decisive in so far as the future sharing of these water resources is concerned. The geographical characteristics of the Golan plateau, the neighbouring areas (both east and west) and their natural drainage system, lend themselves to international cooperation in the control and utilization of the available water resources to the apparent benefit of all sides.

CONCLUSIONS

The delimitation of future peace boundaries between Israel and its neighbours would present extreme difficulties and complexities, the overcoming of which would require much wisdom, generosity, mutual understanding and trust. Equally important is a full objective acquaintance with all the physical and human attributes of the disputed areas as well as those which the boundaries of peace would cross.

Most of the existing boundaries, colonial and post-1948, did not have the benefit when created of an adequate acquaintance with the natural and human environment. Attachment of a status of "holiness" to the colonial boundaries and insistence on their strict preservation are a serious obstacle to the vital necessity for adaptation to new realities, as well as to basic natural factors which were ignored in the past. This rigid attitude was strictly applied under the Egyptian–Israeli peace treaty, which fully restored a colonial Anglo-Turkish boundary and ignored the transformation undergone by parts of the region. Minor exchanges of territory to rectify the course of the boundary in areas which became densely populated would have benefited both sides as well as many of the inhabitants of parts of the frontier zone.

No less important than the determination of the position of the boundaries would be the agreements and arrangements on the actual functions of these peace boundaries. Much of the damage and discomfort caused by the imposition of new boundary lines, or the restoration of old lines which have been obsolete for several decades, may be mitigated by making them zones of contact and cooperation, both at national and local levels. So far, this has only happened to a limited extent to the Egyptian–Israeli peace boundary. This is envisaged for future Israeli–Jordanian boundaries and for those of the Palestinian entity. The creation of boundary lines which would be fully accepted by all sides, to be followed by the administration of the frontier zones and the functions of the boundaries in a manner that would enhance free contacts and cooperation, would be a vital contribution to lasting peace in the Holy Land.

NOTES

1. *Correspondence Respecting the Turco-Egyptian Frontier in the Sinai Peninsula*, Cmd. 3006, London, 1906; *A Report on the Delimitation of the Turco-Egyptian Boundary*, Survey Department, Ministry of Finance, Cairo, 1907; M. Brawer, "Die Neubelebung einer Internationale Grenze auf der Sinai Halbinsel", *Regio Bailiensis*, Vol. XXIV, No. 1 (1983).
2. At that time both Egypt and Palestine were under British control. G. Biger, "The Problem of Determining Palestine's Southern Boundary after World War I", *Ha'mizrakh Ha'khadash* (The New Orient), Vol. 30, No. 1 (1981).
3. Government of Palestine, *Official Gazette*, Special Issue, 1 Sept. 1922, Jerusalem.
4. *Correspondence between C.H. Ley, Director of Survey, and Chief Secretary of the Government of Palestine, 1930–31*, Israel National Archives, Chief Secretary Files, Jerusalem.
5. G. Biger, "Delimitation of Palestine's Eastern Boundary", *Kathedra*, Vol. 20 (1981), Jerusalem (Hebrew).
6. *Agreement Between His Majesty's Government and the French Government Respecting the Boundary Between Syria and Palestine from the Mediterranean to al-Hamma*, Cmd. 1910, London, 1923.
7. M. Brawer, "The Geographical Background of the Jordan Water Dispute", in C.A. Fisher (ed.), *Essays in Political Geography*, London, Methuen, 1968.
8. D. Baram, 'Retsuat Hamat Geder: Skira Geografit' (A Survey of Hamma Strip), Seminar Paper, Department of Geography, Tel-Aviv University, 1974.
9. M. Brawer, "Israel's Northern Boundary and Its Origins", in M. Yedaaya (ed.), *Bémaaravo Shel Hagalil* (The Western Galilee), Haifa, 1970.
10. Y. Cohen, 'Doch Simun Kav Shritat Ha'meshek Bi'rtsuat Aza' (Memorandum on the Delimitation of the Gaza Strip), Israel Defence Army Archives, Tel-Aviv, 1950 (Hebrew).
11. Hashemite Kingdom of Jordan, Department of Statistics, *Census of Population 1961*, Amman (Arabic); Hashemite Kingdom of Jordan, Department of Statistics, *Statistical Yearbooks 1955–1968*, Amman (Arabic); M. Brawer, *The Green Line – The Boundary of the the West Bank*, Tel-Aviv, Tel-Aviv University, 1980. (Hebrew with an English summary).
12. A. Shahar, "The Urban Geography of Jerusalem", in Y. Aviram (ed.), *Yerushalaim Be'khol Ha'dorot* (Jerusalem Throughout Its History), Jerusalem, The Israel Exploration Society, 1968; S.B. Cohen, *Jerusalem – Bridging the Four Walls: A Geopolitical Perspective*, New York, Herzl Press, 1977.
13. J. Schwarz, "Water Resources in Judea, Samaria and the Gaza Strip", in D.J. Elazar, *Judea, Samaria and Gaza: Views on the Present and Future*, Washington, DC, American Enterprise Institute, 1982.
14. M. Benvenisti and S. Khayat, *The West Bank and Gaza Atlas*, The West Bank Data Base Project, Jerusalem, 1988.

15. Ministry of Culture and National Guidance, *Iqlim al-Julan* (The Golan Region), Damascus, 1976; M. Naizal, 'The Israel–Syrian Boundary on the Golan', in A. Degani (ed.), *Ha'gdon Ve'harz Hermon* (The Golan Heights and Mount Hermon), Vol.2, Haifa, University of Haifa, 1993.
16. Y. Tzamir, "The Golan Heights Master Plan", in A. Degani (ed.), *Ha'Golan*.
17. A. Shalev, *Israel and Syria: Peace and Security on the Golan*, Boulder, CO, Westview Press, 1994.

Reassessing the United States– Israeli Special Relationship

BERNARD REICH

> . . . the relationship between the United States and Israel is a
> special relationship for special reasons. It is based upon shared
> interests, shared values, and a shared commitment to
> democracy, pluralism and respect for the individual.
>
> Secretary of State Warren Christopher, February 1993.

THE SIGNING of the Israel–PLO Declaration of Principles (DOP),
celebrated on the White House lawn on 13 September 1993,
ushered in a new era in the politics of the Middle East and changed,
forever and irreversibly, the nature of the Arab–Israeli conflict and of
all of those other factors so inextricably linked to it. The symbolism
of the event and the euphoric and optimistic mood it created over-
shadowed the difficulties in implementing and expanding the agreements that were to follow. It also tended to obscure the fact that,
despite the media event at the White House, the agreement was not the
direct product or outcome of American diplomacy.[1] Nevertheless,
both Israel and the PLO understood the need for the United States to
play the role of host for the signing and, more importantly, for the
donors conference held later. It was clear that the Middle East had been
altered, as demonstrated by this unpredicted conviviality of two long-
time adversaries (as well as their American supporters), but exactly how
and in what ways remained unclear. Delays in implementation and
vocal and often violent opposition within both the Israeli body politic
and the Palestinian camp, in the occupied territories and beyond, soon
marked the process. At the same time it foreshadowed elements of both
continuity and change in the special relationship between the United
States and Israel. Clearly implementation of the process would involve
a series of decisions and actions that would, over time, test the various
components of the covenant between the United States and Israel.

Bernard Reich is Professor of Political Science and International Affairs at George
Washington University. This essay draws from and is based on the author's study of the
United States–Israel relationship to be published shortly by Greenwood Press.

A UNIQUE RELATIONSHIP

The United States and Israel are joined in an unparalleled and complex special relationship aimed at assuring Israel's survival, security and well-being. This special relationship rests on ideological, emotional and moral pillars and on a commitment to democratic principles buttressed by strategic and political factors. Although all bilateral relationships are unique, the United States–Israel relationship is singular in nature, possesses exceptional attributes, and deviates from the norm in United States foreign relations in a positive manner. Shared ideals and values sustain a strong psychological bond between the American and Israeli peoples, as do generally parallel, if not always congruent, political and economic interests. The relationship has endured over decades, surviving numerous crises, and evolving over time from a more or less traditional one into the special relationship of today.[2] It goes well beyond that of military alliances that are built solely on a common hostility to another party and are often marriages of convenience (for example, the anti-Iraq Gulf War coalition of 1990–91) of quite dissimilar parties that would not otherwise have much in common (for example, the United States and Syria).

Despite the positive character of US–Israeli links, perfect congruence of perspective and policy between the two partners is rare and points of discord and difficulty develop from time to time; but these are not permanently damaging and there is a rapid recovery and a return to close ties. Endurance and resilience are trademarks of this special relationship, the hallmark of which is the ability to endure crises in which the parties have conflicting interests. The linkage is intimate and each is involved in the affairs of the other – Israeli envoys enjoy privileged access to the president and other senior American officials, just as Israel's government regularly welcomes American diplomats and numerous visiting dignitaries. Israelis have exploited their access to the congress and their connections with the American Jewish community to influence the nature and direction of US policy, and can identify a measure of achievement in that effort. For its part, the United States has sought, also with some success, to affect the outcome of Israel's elections and the direction of its policies. Americans have an intense interest in developments in and concerning the Jewish state, leading to extensive and detailed media coverage.

The special relationship is also reflected in the laudatory public statements of American officials as well as in the preferential treatment Israel receives from Washington, especially compared to other regional states. The United States and Israel often vote alike in the United Nations and other international bodies.[3] Israel was the first country to have a free-trade area with the United States. Special preferences exist in all areas of interaction, including defence (both the quantity and quality of military assistance, and in other areas), economics (in trade and aid), science and technology, cultural exchange, and diplomatic support (such as UN Security Council vetoes).

Candidates for public office in the United States give Israel disproportionate and positive attention in their position papers and campaign rhetoric. The platforms adopted quadrennially by the major American political parties single out Israel.[4] Israelis have similarly acknowledged the singularity and significance of the relationship with the United States, even while recognizing areas of disagreement.[5]

Although other states have attained a particular significance, none (with the exception of Great Britain and, to an extent, Canada) has achieved the status, over an extended period, of the special position accorded to Israel by American popular opinion and reaffirmed by successive administrations and congresses. Recognition of the interest and of a pro-Israel stance and emotional commitment is widespread and generally accepted, even by those who question it.

A RELATIONSHIP OF MANY STRANDS

Cultural, Religious, and Ideological Affinities

The American commitment to Israel is rooted in strong biblical and historical emotions and ideology, galvanized by shared values and ideals, on the one hand, and feelings of guilt and obligation arising from the Holocaust, on the other. Israel is seen as a like-image state. The underlying factor is democracy, complemented by a common interest in a stable, peaceful and more democratic Middle East in which Israel is accepted and recognized as a legitimate state. The ideological–emotional bond is of long duration but, despite its historical antecedents in the early days of the American experience, it was only after the 1967 Six Day War that it achieved its key position in the American mind.

Americans have traditionally been sympathetic towards peoples striving for nationhood and independence, and towards persecuted peoples in particular, which inclined them to look with favour on the aspirations of Jewish nationalism. The Zionist claims received a wide hearing because of the presence of millions of Jews in the United States, and encountered greater receptivity because of their association with the Bible and its prophecies. Support for Israel derived from a guilt complex but also served as a means to make amends for a terrible tragedy; a Jewish state provided a welcome place of refuge for the survivors of the Holocaust. President Harry Truman and others clearly saw the need to support the creation of Israel in part as a reaction to the "guilt" factor resulting from the Holocaust and the extermination of six million Jews by Nazi Germany. Truman identified a moral responsibility to honour an obligation, derived from the Balfour Declaration, that focused on the establishment of a Jewish state in Palestine.

Israel's special place in American thinking antedates its emergence as a state. Manifestations of support for the aspirations of the Jewish people to return to Zion can be traced to President John Adams. Woodrow Wilson believed that this not only involved the "rebirth of the Jewish people", but also the potential for new ideals and ethical values for mankind that would spring from having the Jews restored to their land. He endorsed the Balfour Declaration of 1917, as did the congress and individual senators and congressmen, together with numerous state governments and legislatures.[6] Such support was rooted in the influence of the Old Testament on the Founding Fathers and the spiritual legacy they provided to succeeding generations. The Christian American religious heritage helps to secure a link to the land and people of Israel. Religious faith later became a factor in support for the State of Israel. American political leaders identified a religious component in their decision-making. Truman saw the Jews deriving a legitimate historical right to Palestine from the Old Testament and would cite biblical verses to support that view. Lyndon Johnson told B'nai B'rith in September 1968: "Most, if not all of you, have very deep ties with the land and with the people of Israel, as I do, for my Christian faith sprang from yours. The Bible stories are woven into my child-hood memories as the gallant struggle of modern Jews to be free of persecution is also woven into our souls."[7]

The American evangelical movement provides strong grassroots support for Israel. Fundamentalist Christians are deeply committed on religious grounds to the concept of a homeland for the Jews in their ancestral territory and to support for Israel. Israel is seen as a fulfilment of biblical prophecy – the Old and New Testaments predict the return of the Jews to the Holy Land and the creation of a Jewish state in Israel before the second coming of Christ.

On top of these religious factors, there is a broad affinity between the United States and Israel. There is an element of cultural similarity that identifies Israel as a "Western" state among "oriental" entities and as a perpetuator of the Judaeo-Christian heritage. Americans have felt a strong empathy for Israel as a free and open democratic society, imbued with the liberal values and humanistic culture of the West; it is identified as a model worthy of emulation.[8] The Israeli democracy did not evolve from an authoritarian form of government nor was it forced upon it; Israel is an inherently democratic state whose concepts and institutions were derived from the Zionist movement and the Jewish community in Palestine (*Yishuv*) during the British Mandate. The United States has had an interest in the survival of the relatively few democratic states already in existence, and Bill Clinton stressed democratic values in his election campaign. "Democracy has always been our nation's perfecting impulse", he stated. "Democracy abroad also protects our own concrete economic and security interests here at home."[9] These perceptions and shared values continue to undergird the US–Israel relationship, despite an evolution in how each element is perceived and forms a part of the whole.

The Strategic Imperative

Interestingly enough, strategic considerations were conspicuously absent in the early stages of the US–Israeli relationship. Although the United States was the first country to recognize Israel, President Truman's support for the creation of a Jewish state was not motivated by Israel's strategic value to the United States nor was he dissuaded by the argument that it was a strategic liability.[10] He supported the United Nations Partition Resolution of November 1947 and the consequent creation of a Jewish State in Palestine (that is, Israel) primarily for humanitarian and associated reasons. The pleas of Chaim Weizmann had impressed him, and he also considered the domestic American political factor (that is, the American Jewish vote).

A close strategic connection did not follow the creation of Israel; the developing relationship was rooted in ideological–emotional factors. The United States provided virtually no aid during Israel's War of Independence or in the years immediately following; indeed, after Israel's independence there were strong pressures on President Truman to avoid a regional policy that included Israel and to resist Israel's requests for economic and military aid. The United States developed a policy that relied on the Arab states to confront the Soviet Union, from which Israel was generally excluded.[11]

The US role as an arms supplier evolved from that of non-participant (the United States adopted an arms embargo in 1947) to that of principal supplier of modern, sophisticated military equipment, beginning in the late 1960s.[12] Some military equipment was sold earlier, but the Kennedy administration inaugurated the first significant weapons sales with Hawk anti-aircraft missiles in 1962. During the Six Day War the United States provided tangential support for Israel but did not play a direct role – it did not engage in combat or resupply Israel, though it moved the Sixth Fleet to counter a potential Soviet intervention and supported Israel's position in the United Nations by opposing Soviet initiatives there. Lyndon Johnson's 19 June 1967 speech enunciating principles for peace in the Middle East established a framework for post-war diplomacy. Nevertheless, restraint continued to characterize US–Israel relations in the strategic realm even after Israel's astounding victory over its Arab foes. During the Nixon tenure, US arms transfers grew significantly and the United States played an important supportive role during and after the October 1973 War. Despite the Camp David Accords and the Egypt–Israel Peace Treaty, the US–Israel strategic connection was not greatly expanded during the Carter administration.[13] Israel's dependence on the United States for arms increased, but its role as an ally was not enhanced.

It was only during the Reagan administration that overt strategic cooperation between the United States and Israel developed, as instability and insecurity became commonplace in the Persian Gulf and Southwest Asia. Already before assuming office, Ronald Reagan had made public his own view of the special relationship:

> American policy-makers downgrade Israel's geopolitical importance as a stabilizing force, as a deterrent to radical hegemony and as a military offset to the Soviet Union. The fall of Iran has increased Israel's value as perhaps the only remaining strategic asset in the region on which the United States can truly rely; other pro-Western states in the region, especially Saudi Arabia and the smaller Gulf kingdoms, are weak and vulnerable.[14]

He identified Israel as "a major strategic asset to America. Israel is not a client, but a very reliable friend."

President Reagan's ideas often coincided with those of the Begin government in Israel, although they were not usually shared by the professional levels in the Department of Defense. Reagan sought to reassure Menachem Begin in a letter made public on 16 February 1982, in which he articulated his view of Israel's security: "I am determined to see that Israel's qualitative technological edge is maintained and am mindful as well of your concerns with respect to quantitative factors and their impact upon Israel's security."[15]

Indeed, during the 1980s Israel increasingly came to be viewed as a strategic asset and the only reliable ally of the United States in the Middle East by Ronald Reagan, as well as other policy-makers, congressmen and public officials. US economic and military assistance rose to $3 billion annually, all of it in grants, and was supplemented by millions more from special arrangements. Strategic cooperation became the catch-phrase of those who argued that Israel could be useful in supporting US interests throughout the Middle East, including the Persian Gulf and the Arabian Peninsula. Nevertheless, many American policy-makers and strategic planners saw this as impractical, recognizing few circumstances in which Israel's participation would be invited or even welcomed.[16]

Still, by the end of Reagan's second term there were numerous areas of military cooperation that went beyond those spelled out in formal memoranda of understanding. An American declaratory policy that openly embraced Israel as an "ally", and often underscored the United States commitment to Israel's security, buttressed the relationship. But the pattern of strategic cooperation established in the Reagan administration did not expand during the Bush presidency. It was tested during the international crisis and war spawned by Iraq's invasion of Kuwait in August 1990. The United States asked Israel to keep a low profile that would avoid giving Saddam Hussein a tool with which to split the anti-Iraq coalition, and when President Bush asked that Israel not respond to the Iraqi Scud attacks Israel complied. At the same time, the administration turned to other regional states, especially Turkey and Egypt, for both military forces and logistical support.

Whatever Israel's strategic value to the United States may have been before the end of the cold war and the demise of the Soviet bloc, and eventually the Soviet state itself, the situation has clearly changed with these momentous developments. However, US–Israeli strategic co-operation never was premised solely on countering the Soviet threat; both states took a broader approach, despite the relatively narrow wording of their formal agreements. Besides, the disintegration of the Soviet Union was clearly of greater concern to and more traumatic for the Arab states which lost their primary armourer and diplomatic-political advocate. For Israel, this development reduced the threat – but essentially an indirect one.[17]

Commitment to Israel's Existence

Since Israel's independence, the United States has had an interest in its survival and security, although this has not always been a priority focus of US policy. The underlying arguments have concentrated on shared values and historical association, but there has also been strategic utility and intangible values. According to Henry Kissinger,

> There's a moral commitment to Israel which does not derive from the fact that it is a strategic asset even though it is *also* a strategic asset. Because when all is said and done, it is the one country which we can be sure will never change its friendship for the United States, and which in a foreseeable crisis represents a relationship of fundamental strategic importance.[18]

And President Carter spoke in the same vein in a press conference on 12 May 1977:

> We have a special relationship with Israel. It's absolutely crucial that no one in our country or around the world ever doubt that our No. 1 commitment in the Middle East is to protect the right of Israel to exist, to exist permanently, and to exist in peace. It's a special relationship.[19]

Yet although there is a widely perceived commitment to Israel's survival and security, the nature of that commitment and the means to implement it, beyond providing diplomatic and political support and military and economic assistance, remain ambiguous. The commitment has been couched in the generalized form of presidential statements rather than formal accords. While such statements reaffirmed the American interest in supporting the political independence and territorial integrity of Middle Eastern states, including Israel, they do not commit the United States to specific actions in particular circumstances.

Israel has no mutual security treaty with the United States, nor is it a member of any alliance system requiring the United States to take up arms on its behalf. It is assumed that the United States would come to Israel's assistance were it to be gravely threatened, but there is no assurance that it will do so, even though the US–Israeli relationship has been codified to some extent in specific documents associated with the 1975 Egyptian–Israeli Disengagement Agreement (Sinai II), the Egypt–Israel Peace Treaty process, the 1981 US–Israeli Memorandum of Understanding on Strategic Cooperation, and subsequent similar arrangements. Sinai II and the Egyptian–Israeli Peace Treaty (1979), particularly the accompanying US–Israel letters and memoranda, placed the American role on a more precise footing.[20] The United States commitment centred on the survival of Israel against implacable enemies. This led Israeli decision-makers to believe that the United States would not permit a major Soviet military action against it, and would act to deter the Soviets from becoming significantly involved in a regional conflict, but Israeli leaders were not similarly certain about the nature and extent of United States support of its position in an Arab–Israeli context. Although they believed that the United States would ensure Israel's security and integrity they did not interpret the commitment too broadly.

Has the US commitment to Israel changed since the end of the cold war? Despite the changes that have occurred in the nature of the threat to Israel's security, the commitment appears as strong as it was during the cold war era. In April 1990, the-then Congressman Les Aspin addressed the question of whether, given the changes in East–West relations, US–Israeli relations were likely to diminish. Having noted that in the 1980s the United States had signed three formal agreements with Israel and that President Reagan had issued a national security decision directive establishing a joint political–military group, and having listed a wide range of cooperative strategic and military efforts, Aspin concluded that "quite simply, the demise of the cold war should not change our strategic relationship with Israel". He argued that the relationship was not premised on the Soviet threat to Israel but rather on the latter's strategic needs to cope with the Arab threat, and that it was based on America's strategic needs that had not involved any Soviet threat in the Middle East in recent years.[21]

The United States remains committed to the survival and security of Israel, preferably without a direct commitment of American forces.[22] Thus it has been American policy to provide the arms and related materiel essential for the Israel Defence Forces (IDF) to ensure the survival and security of the Jewish state. Increasingly this has been subsumed under the rubric of "maintaining Israel's qualitative edge" over its Arab adversaries.

Pursuing this policy will pose challenges for American ingenuity because of its perception that the Arabs require sophisticated arms for their own security and that it is in the best interests of the United States to supply such arms, not least since these sales are important for the US economy. The United States thus will increasingly find itself in the position of providing equipment to the Arab states and of then having to compensate Israel to assure its qualitative edge. For Israel to oppose United States arms sales to the Arab states is likely increasingly to prove futile. Arms sales clearly affect the regional military balance, but opposition to such sales runs into the hard facts of economic necessity in the United States. Instead, Israel will need to focus its efforts on security compensatory arms supply to sustain its qualitative edge.[23] For its part, even as it pursues efforts to achieve an Arab–Israeli peace, the United States will sustain the strategic links that ensure Israel's survival and security through military supply and maintaining the qualitative edge in order to achieve peace and reduce the threats to the broader US interests in the Middle East.

Despite some concerns about the United States as a wholly reliable partner, Israel still views the United States as the essential element in ensuring its survival and security, in maintaining its strategic qualitative edge, and in potentially guaranteeing a peace agreement with its Arab neighbours. The special relationship, with all its flaws, remains essential to Israel's survival and security. As the then Assistant Secretary of State for South Asian and Near Eastern Affairs (and later Ambassador to Israel), Edward Djerejian, put it in June 1992: "Our differences should not obscure . . . the fact that the US and Israel share fundamental values and that we remain unshakeably committed to Israel's security and to preserving Israel's qualitative edge over any likely combination of aggressors."[24]

THE UNITED STATES AND THE ARAB-ISRAELI PEACE PROCESS

This pledge is particularly instructive, given the fact that the Bush administration's relationship with Israel was less positive than that of the Reagan tenure. Existing differences on such issues as settlement construction in the occupied territories and the role of the Palestinians in the peace process were further exacerbated following the Gulf War, as the United States pressed for progress on an Arab–Israeli peace process. Although there was unanimity on the desirability of peace between Israel and its neighbours, the Israeli government was not convinced that the Arab world was ready to move towards peace, and the pressures on Israel to participate were not always accompanied by the pledges and reassurances that, in the past, had often persuaded it to negotiate despite scepticism concerning its interlocutors' motives. This was compounded by the high profile public clash of the administration with the Israeli government and the pro-Israel lobby in the autumn of 1991 on housing loan guarantees.

Israel under Yitzhak Shamir's right-wing government, concerned with both procedure and substance, approached the Madrid peace conference in 1991 with trepidation. The United States, for its part, was determined to convene a conference and was less troubled by Israel's objections. Yet Israel managed to impose conditions, in exchange for its participation, especially concerning the Palestinian role. Substantive differences between the United States and Israel since 1967 have focused on the interpretation of United Nations Security Council Resolution 242; while both agree that the resolution does not require Israel's total withdrawal from the occupied territories (which the legislative history supports), they have differed on the extent of withdrawal and whether it is required on all fronts (the Sinai Peninsula, the Golan Heights, the West Bank, and the Gaza Strip). Israel rejected the concept of insubstantial alterations, articulated by Secretary of State William Rogers in 1969, to refer to minor changes in the 1967 frontiers between Israel and the occupied territories, because it did not comport well with Israel's conception of required adjustments. The immediate problem, however, revolved around the continuation of Israeli settlement activity in the occupied territories (which in the United States' view include East Jerusalem), deemed by the Shamir government as a legitimate right of Jews in the Land of Israel and by the Bush administration as both illegal and an obstacle to peace. In the words of Secretary of State James Baker: "I don't think that there is any bigger obstacle to peace than the settlement activity that continues not only unabated but at an enhanced pace."[25]

The complexities of the United States–Israel relationship and the peace process became apparent again in early January 1992, as the former joined in a United Nations Security Council resolution condemning Israel for deporting Palestinian activists to Lebanon after a series of terrorist attacks against Israelis in the occupied territories and in Israel proper. Israel read the US action as a modification of policy that raised doubts about the role that the United States might play in the peace process.[26]

Israelis recognize that the United States must play a role in initiating and facilitating a peace process to resolve the conflict and to gain Israel's acceptance in the region. This, however, does not mean that the process proposed by the United States or the content of American policies on specific elements of the dispute will be those necessarily preferred by Israel. In any event, Israel views the United States as the facilitator, not the maker, of peace; in the Israeli perception peacemaking is a function of the parties to the conflict rather than the domain of the international community or the "only remaining superpower".

The Israel–PLO Declaration of Principles illustrates this point. Though the negotiations were conducted in secrecy and Norway played the crucial role of host and facilitator, the signing ceremony on 13 September 1993 took place in Washington, as did the donors conference designed to secure the funds to implement the first phases of the agreement. Once again this demonstrated the centrality of the United States in the peace process. It was only the United States that could secure the handshake between Rabin and Arafat and play the crucial role of sustaining the momentum of the process thereafter, despite numerous challenges to it. For Israel the combination of American involvement and the reassurance that Israeli security and well-being would be sustained made the continuation of the process possible. Clearly an Israel ready to move towards peace could only be a country confident of the special relationship with the United States that provided its ultimate guarantee of security as it made concessions for peace.[27] For the PLO and the Arab states the US special relationship with Israel gave it a role that could not be usurped by any other state for only the United States could secure the required actions from Israel.

NOT A LIABILITY

This latter point demonstrates that while Israel has not been an unalloyed asset, neither has there been a palpable negative effect on the United States role in the Arab world because of its connection to Israel. Contrary to long-standing suggestions that there is an either/or choice between Israel and the Arab states (or, often, Arab oil), developments have shown that there is no requirement for such a decision. The "Israeli connection" has not precluded relationships with the Arab states, nor has it necessarily compromised the quality of those links. On the contrary, US–Israeli ties have illustrated the overall value and reliability of American commitments, including those in the Arab world.

The special relationship has also reinforced the position of the United States as the only viable external factor in the quest for an Arab–Israeli peace. Washington's intervention was crucial in achieving the cease-fire agreements in the Israeli–Arab wars of 1967, 1970 and 1973, and in obtaining the disengagement agreements between Israel and Egypt and Israel and Syria in 1974, the Sinai II accord in 1975, the Camp David Accords in 1978, the Egypt–Israel Peace Treaty in 1979, the cease-fire that ended the Lebanon War in 1982, the 17 May 1983 agreement between Israel and Lebanon, the convening of the Madrid Peace Conference of 1991, and the sustaining of the subsequent bilateral and multilateral negotiations. And, of course, in the wake of the Oslo talks, it was the United States to which Israel and the PLO turned to assure implementation of the DOP. The US relationship with Israel was instrumental in generating the level of regional influence needed to broker these processes, that was never attained by the anti-Israel and pro-Arab Soviet Union (despite the visibility as co-chairman often granted it by the United States, the Soviets and, now, the Russians, were and are informed about, but not significantly involved in, the peace process) nor by the more neutral European Community.

Notwithstanding Arab hostility to Israel, the United States has increasingly strengthened its links with the Arab world. Arab states accept US aid, purchase American military equipment, receive US technical assistance, and, despite the Arab boycott of Israel, do substantial business with, and sell oil to, the United States and other friends and allies of Israel. The special relationship has had no significant adverse effect on America's access to Middle Eastern oil, with the exception of the 1973 oil embargo. There is no reason to believe that even if Israel were to disappear this would result in a significant reduction in the price of oil or a meaningful increase in access to the region's petroleum resources.

Many of the Arab (and Muslim) states appear to be reconciled to the United States connection with Israel, despite continuous, and sometimes vigorous and visible, protests of Israel's policies and of American support of them. For some there is the recognition of the reality of the New World Order. With the Soviet Union out of the picture, it is clear that the United States represents the only realistic source of economic and military assistance and political–diplomatic support. The 1991 Gulf War drove this point home. King Hussein of Jordan appeared to recognize this factor in re-orientating his policies after the end of the war, as did Hafiz al-Asad in committing Syria to participate in the United States-sponsored peace process and in his desire for an enhanced dialogue with the Clinton administration.

THE DYNAMICS OF COLLABORATION AND DISCORD

The expectation that any alliance or special relationship should be marked by a wholly congruent and symmetric set of positions and policies is unrealistic. Friction is a component of relationships, even among close allies. Strains between the United States and Israel have parallels in America's relationships with its NATO allies and other states with which it has formal treaties of alliance. In recent years, the United States has had high profile clashes over political and economic issues with Canada, Japan, Germany, France and the European Community. It has engaged in sometimes acrimonious debate on defence burden-sharing and other strategic issues with both NATO and Japan. At times its friends and allies have opposed American initiatives, such as the reflagging of ships in the Persian Gulf, the air raid against Libya, and actions concerning Bosnia. The US–Israel relationship, too, has witnessed such traumas as the pressure by the Eisenhower administration during the Suez crisis in 1956–57, the Rogers Plan of December 1969, the reassessment of 1975, and the confrontation over loan guarantees in 1991–92.

The differences between the United States and Israel, however, are akin to those within a family: they focus on tactics and policy, but not on fundamentals. The special relationship has been replete with broad areas of agreement and numerous examples of discord over more than four-and-a-half decades. Broad agreement and understanding and a generalized commitment to peace exist, and specific questions and issues have been approached within that framework. It is concerning specifics that the relationship has often had its episodes of disagreement, with each party assiduously seeking to influence the actions of the other. The two states maintain general accord on interests and policy goals – including the need to prevent war, to resolve the Arab–Israeli conflict, and to sustain Israel's survival and security. But as the bilateral dialogue has increasingly dealt with details there have been disturbances, sometimes serious, in the relationship. Strains are inevitable given the extensive nature of the issues that will be considered in the dialogue.

There were, are and will be, divergences that derive from differences of perspective and in policy environments. The United States has broad concerns resulting from its global responsibilities. Israel's more restricted regional environment, the hostility and threat found within it, and its lesser responsibilities, condition that state's perspective. The asymmetries between the two states – their different sizes, places in the world order, and global outlooks – certainly play a part. Most significant, however, are the differences of expectations. For Israel, the relationship – especially the strategic connection – is vital; the United States is Israel's primary source of military equipment, as well as of political and diplomatic support. Their economic links are fundamental to Israel's economic health. For the United States, however, the relationship is far less significant. Measured in conventional terms, Israel is of limited military or economic importance to the

United States; its status as a democratic state commends it to the United States, but it is not a strategically vital state, nor is it likely to emerge as one.

Divergence on methods and techniques has ranged widely, from the appropriate form of response to Arab terrorism, to the value of great power efforts to resolve the conflict; from the appropriateness and timing of face-to-face and direct Arab–Israeli negotiations, to the provision (types, quantities and timing) of essential military supplies. The two states have disagreed on Israel's reprisals to Arab actions. They have had major differences concerning the occupied territories, their status and Israel's role there, including the building of settlements. And they do not approach the issue of Jerusalem from consonant positions. They have argued over Israel's desire for significant changes in the pre-Six Day War armistice lines as contrasted with the United States insistence on "insubstantial alterations" or "minor modifications".

Personality clashes between senior American and Israeli officials have also affected the tenor of the relationship. This was particularly evident in the relations between Jimmy Carter and Menachem Begin. During the Reagan administration mutual dislike and mistrust extended further, as various officials were unhappy with Begin and Sharon; Israelis, in turn, were anxious about Secretary of Defense Caspar Weinberger's policies. The clash between Yitzhak Shamir on the one hand, and George Bush and James Baker, on the other, was perhaps the most obvious.

There are limits on policy and decisions, but there are also self-imposed limits in the dealings of states, and these apply in the case of the United States–Israel relationship. There are limits to concessions that are possible despite extensive pressures. Israel will not "give in" on certain points, even under extensive pressure, and United States' efforts to induce changes in Israel's positions generally are cognizant of the limits beyond which it will achieve little, if any, policy modifications. Core values and elements identified as matters of vital national interest are not susceptible to modification through influence. As noted by Yitzhak Shamir: "On the fundamental life-and-death issues – such as security, Jerusalem, the 1967 borders, the danger of a Palestinian state – we have no choice but to stand by our position firmly, strongly and clearly – even against our great friend the United States."[28] Similar perspectives are regularly articulated by Rabin and his ministers.

Finally, it should be noted that Israeli decision-makers often respond to direct pressures with resentment and defiance. Pressure is an unacceptable interference in Israel's sovereign decision-making process and hence counter-productive. Israel will not rely on the wisdom of others on matters of vital national interest, and overt efforts to exert such influence are doomed to failure. Because of this sensitivity, and because American decision-makers have understood it, the United States has often pursued the path of reassurance, indicating it would not use pressure to generate changes in Israeli policies, and providing tangible evidence of its support through military and economic aid and political and diplomatic action.

In assessing the special relationship, however, it is important to distinguish between the basic underlying linkages and the ephemeral issues. The former remains essentially constant, while the latter is constantly shifting. It is the changes in the facade that are generally reported in the media and dominate public perceptions of the connection. Behind the facade lie the fundamentals – basic shared values, the enduring place of Israel in the "mind of America," and strategic and political elements. At the core is the unique commitment on the part of the United States to the security of the Jewish state and the conviction that progress towards the peaceful resolution of the Arab–Israeli conflict is in the American interest. Periods of misunderstanding, friction and confrontation, sometimes lengthy, sometimes brief, often alternate with periods of harmony and agreement.

During the spring of 1992, in the wake of the failure of Israel's efforts to secure loan guarantees, and with charges that Israel had misused American military technology, the relationship was marked by bitter recriminations, tension and stress. By the summer, after the Israeli Knesset elections, a euphoric mood dominated the bilateral relationship as Yitzhak Rabin became prime minister, and predictions of "sweetness and light" replaced an atmosphere of gloom. Former Foreign Minister Abba Eban has described this roller-coaster relationship: "One day they would pat you on the back and the next day kick you in the face."[29] It is a pendulum effect that fluctuates between the narrow confines imposed by their unique linkage.

NEW WORLD ORDER, ENDURING RELATIONSHIP

Relationships between friends and allies vary in quality and intensity over time. Even the most vaunted of the special relationships, that between the United States and Great Britain, has recently been called into question due to personal and policy differences between Prime Minister John Major and President Clinton. So, too, have there been similar factors affecting the warmth and robustness of the United States special relationship with Israel. The world has changed and become more complex, and with that alteration the relevance and strength of the linkage between the United States and Israel has also been modified. Nevertheless, despite personal suspicion and animus that will surface from time to time, and despite policy differences resulting from divergent perspectives on important decisions that will develop, the two partners will survive these and other storms in their dealings and will continue to be connected in a special relationship which stresses the positive elements of their links in the areas of central importance to each. Israel's survival and security, and its quest for peace, will retain their centrality in American policy, and Israel's commitment to the democratic (or "free") world, coupled with its espousal of free market economic systems, and predicated on a long-standing historically and religiously-based moral connection, will continue to assure the linkage to an American government that places these values at the core of its system. American military and economic assistance to ensure these objectives will continue to be an important element of the strategic connection (with modification to reflect the economic reality of the context in which policy decisions are made), and a meaningful measure of the relationship. The moral underpinnings of their connection and the confidence that they have established in each other is likely to continue to outweigh the crises that have and will develop in their relations. In the final analysis, the numerous links which bind them together will outweigh the often ephemeral issues and concerns that have worked to separate Washington and Jerusalem.

The confluence of interests, and the willingness to pool resources and efforts to achieve and secure them, has varied over time – it was somewhat easier to speak of a strategic relationship when there was also a mutually-shared suspicion of Soviet policies and machinations in the Middle East; nevertheless, even in the post-cold war era there remains a considerable overlap of core concerns (such as an Arab–Israeli peace, the security and well-being of Israel, and regional stability) on which they can work together. This special relationship will continue to flourish in part because of a hospitable and supportive domestic environment, an outgrowth of the symbiotic interaction among the American Jewish community, public opinion, and the congress, that has no precise parallel in other bilateral relationships. Episodes of discord in the formal relationship carried out by the executives of the two states have often been limited by the safety net provided to Israel by a sympathetic congress buoyed by favourable public opinion and influenced by an activist Jewish community and pro-Israel lobby. Also, these same elements have helped to expand the bilateral relation-ship by sustaining numerous interactions at the unofficial level and by encouraging the executive branch to expand official links. Alterations in the policy environment and shifts in personnel have generated nuances of change in specific instances, and these will continue; but the overall reliability of congress, public opinion, and the Israel lobby (with the Jewish community at its core), retains its basic importance.

Until a comprehensive peace is achieved between Israel and the

Arabs, the bilateral special relationship between the United States and Israel is unlikely to be dramatically altered by the extensive shifts in the international system caused by the demise of the Soviet Union and the end of the cold war, or by the modifications in the Middle Eastern regional system associated with the Gulf War; not even by the process (initiated by Madrid and the DOP) of moving towards a comprehensive and lasting peace. The bilateral relationship has never been cold war based, neither in its origins nor in its continuity. The Soviet–American competition was, for some of the period after the Six Day War, a factor further expanding the strategic connection, but it was not its basis. Israel's focus on its survival and security, and consequently on the military balance and its need for arms acquisition, concentrated on the regional equilibrium, not on the Soviet factor.

Ultimately, in the bilateral special relationship, Israel will meet the tests of strategic utility and shared values as will the United States. The United States must sustain its special relationship and commitment to the survival and security of its democratic partner. In a world in which the United States dotes on emerging democracies and seeks to promote such democratic values worldwide, assuring the future of a state that is accountable to its people and transfers power through orderly and peaceful change, is a logical priority. The two states, however, will continue to disagree over many of the specifics and the connection will be marked by both euphoria and despair as in the past; they will diverge on many aspects of the regional situation and on the broader international environment and the appropriate policies to respond to them, while retaining common views on the need for peace and stability in the Middle East and for the survival and security of Israel.

Relations between the United States and Israel will continue to be viewed, discussed, analysed, and determined with a passion reserved for few other connections. Israel and its special relationship with the United States remain controversial subjects of intense debate and discussion, although its survival and security are the irreducible minimums even for the American critics of the state and its links with the United States.

Differences and discord, tensions, and even occasional clashes, cannot obscure the fact that the covenant established between the United States and Israel defines a special relationship, both in form and in substance, that is likely to be sustained into the twenty-first century. In the words of Vice President Al Gore:

> We have deepened and strengthened our relationship to the point where it is probably the closest that we have with any of our friends and allies anywhere in the world . . . we support Israel because it is our major democratic ally with strategic and ideological and

cultural ties that grow stronger each year . . . as we work to achieve the goal of peace in the Middle East, we are guided by the fundamental principle which forms the basis for the peace process: our absolute commitment to Israel's security and to close US–Israel relations . . . The security of Israel is important to us, and we make no bones about it . . . The US stands by Israel in an unshakeable partnership for peace.[30]

NOTES

1. Although both Israel and the United States have worked hard to argue that the Oslo talks and the DOP were a result of the Madrid-initiated Arab–Israeli peace process, the fact remains that the United States did not initiate nor participate in the Oslo process nor was it central to the post-signing negotiations, despite its crucial role in rallying international support and securing international financing for the DOP and its implementation. On the contrary, it can be argued that the Oslo process succeeded precisely because the US-brokered and sponsored process in Washington was not marked by any significant breakthrough, leaving the parties to seek alternative channels.
2. Some of the unique features of the United States–Israel relationship developed early (for example, the shared values), but others (such as the strategic connection) came only later.
3. Israel's voting pattern on major issues often has the highest correspondence with that of the United States of any United Nations member.
4. For example, the 1992 Democratic Party platform noted: "The end of the Cold War does not alter America's deep interest in our long-standing special relationship with Israel, based on shared values, a mutual commitment to democracy, and a strategic alliance that benefits both nations." The Republican Party platform acknowledged "Israel's demonstrated strategic importance to the United States, as our most reliable and capable ally in this part of the world . . . [and] the only true democracy in the Middle East."
5. In presenting his government to the Knesset in July 1992, Prime Minister Yitzhak Rabin noted: "Sharing with us in the making of peace will also be the United States, whose friendship and special closeness we prize. We shall spare no effort to strengthen and improve the special relationship we have with the one power in the world." Embassy of Israel, Washington, DC, *For Your Information*, "Presentation of the New Government: Address before Knesset by Prime Minister Designate Yitzhak Rabin, 13 July 1992", n.p.
6. In 1922 the congress adopted unanimously the Lodge–Fish resolution that supported a "national home".
7. "B'nai B'rith: The President's Remarks at the 125th Anniversary Meeting, September 10, 1968", *Weekly Compilation of Presidential Documents*, 16 Sept. 1968, p.1343. Jimmy Carter recalls: "In my affinity for Israel, I shared the sentiment of most other Southern Baptists . . . The Judaeo-Christian ethic and study of the Bible were bonds between Jews and Christians which had always been part of my life. I also believed very deeply that the Jews who had survived the Holocaust deserved their own nation, and that they had a right to live in peace among their neighbours. I considered this homeland for the Jews to be compatible with the teachings of the Bible, hence ordained by God. These moral and religious beliefs made my commitment to the security of Israel unshakeable." Jimmy Carter, *Keeping Faith: Memoirs of a President*, New York, Bantam Books, 1982, p.274.
8. See, for example, Address by Vice President Mondale to the American Jewish Committee, New York, 18 May 1978.
9. "Democracy in America", Remarks by Governor Bill Clinton, University of Wisconsin, Milwaukee, Wisconsin, 1 October 1992, transcript, p.1. Israel was among his examples of a "democratic ally". His argument rests on several elements: "Democratic countries do not go to war with one another. They don't sponsor terrorism, or threaten one another with weapons of mass destruction. Precisely because they are more likely to respect civil liberties, property rights, and the rule of law within their own borders, democracies provide the best foundations on which to build international order.

Democracies make more reliable partners in diplomacy and trade, and in protecting the global environment." Ibid., pp.3–4.

10. Those in his administration, such as Secretary of Defense James Forrestal, who were focused on strategic considerations advised Truman that the oil resources and the size of the Arab world were of greater significance to the United States than an independent Jewish state. They argued that US support of a Jewish state would be a strategic liability, that there would be significant and irreparable damage to American interests (especially in the oil sector) in the Middle East and the Muslim world, and that such a move would entail "worldwide repercussions".

11. The proposal for a Middle East Defence Command (1951) saw Egypt as the centrepiece, with Israel excluded, and the Baghdad Pact (1955) and the Eisenhower Doctrine (1957) were also Arab-focused.

12. By the time of the Suez Crisis in 1956, Israel was already seeking arms from the West to counter-balance Soviet Bloc provisions to the Arab states, particularly Egypt. France, not the United States, became the dominant supplier of military equipment. Israel's efforts to secure a defence pact with Washington were rebuffed. Only after 1967 was the anti-Soviet fervour of the United States channelled into strategic cooperation with Israel.

13. Nevertheless, Jimmy Carter wrote in his memoirs: "For the well-being of my own country, I wanted the Middle East region stable and at peace; I did not want to see Soviet influence expanded in the area. In its ability to help accomplish these purposes, Israel was a strategic asset to the United States." Carter, *Keeping Faith*, pp.274–75.

14. *Washington Post*, 15 Aug. 1979.

15. For the text of the letter see, *New York Times*, 17 Feb. 1982.

16. Some believed that Israel was a limited and perhaps flawed asset, as demonstrated by the decision not to use its facilities for the evacuation of wounded marines after the Beirut massacre of 1983; by the idea of creating a Jordanian, not Israeli, rapid deployment force for regional contingencies; and by efforts to build facilities for pre-positioning US military equipment at Ras Banas in Egypt rather than use Israeli facilities.

17. Direct Soviet–Israeli conflict had been severely limited and officially unacknowledged, occurring primarily during the late stages of the Egyptian-Israeli War of Attrition, in the spring and early summer of 1970.

18. Quoted in *Jerusalem Post*, 6 Jan. 1981.

19. *New York Times*, 13 May 1977.

20. For example, the memorandum of agreement between the government of Israel and the United States, dated 1 September 1975, that accompanied the Sinai II accords and was signed by Secretary of State Henry Kissinger and Israeli Deputy Prime Minister and Minister of Foreign Affairs Yigal Allon, stated: "In view of the long-standing United States commitment to the survival and security of Israel, the United States Government will view with particular gravity threats to Israel's security or sovereignty by a world power. In support of this objective, the United States Government will in the event of such threat consult promptly with the Government of Israel with respect to what support, diplomatic or otherwise, or assistance it can lend to Israel in accordance with its constitutional practices." Accompanying the Egypt–Israel Peace Treaty of 1979 were memoranda of agreement that reaffirmed and broadened the abovementioned assurances, including economic and military assistance and assurance of Israel's oil requirements.

21. Congressman Les Aspin in "The Soref Symposium: The Middle East in an Era of Changing Superpower Relations", Washington, DC, The Washington Institute for Near East Policy, 1990, pp.39–45 (citation from p.40).

22. Israelis continue to be sceptical of international security guarantees. While recognizing and appreciating the contributions made by the United States to their survival and security, they sustain the long-held view that they do not seek American troops to assure their security. Israel continues to see its security assured by its own forces and not by outside powers, including the United States. While seeking military and economic assistance as tangible expressions of the American commitment, Israel has been particularly adamant about its long held policy of self-reliance. The dangers inherent in direct American participation have been recognized and this judgement appears validated by American experiences in overseas military involvements. Vietnam-analogous situations cause discomfort in Israel's decision-making circles. The exceptional instance of a small number of Americans operating Patriot missile batteries in Israel during the Gulf war has not altered the doctrine of self-reliance.

23. The decision by President Bush to sell 72 F-15 aircraft to Saudi Arabia in 1992 is a case in point. Prime Minister Rabin opposed the sale on grounds that it would adversely affect Israel's security, but he understood that despite Israel's opposition the sale would go forward for economic reasons, so he sought to avoid provoking a political controversy. Thus, Israel lodged a pro forma protest with the US and concentrated on securing pledged compensation in order to strengthen its own capabilities in the development and production of essential defence equipment.
24. Testimony before the Subcommittee on Europe and the Middle East of the House Foreign Affairs Committee on 24 June 1992.
25. Testimony before the Subcommittee on Foreign Operations of the House Appropriations Committee, 22 May 1991.
26. For a detailed exposition of Israel's views see Bernard Reich, "Israeli Perceptions of the Peace Process", *The World and I*, Vol.7 (April 1992), pp.500–517.
27. In a joint press conference with Prime Minister Yitzhak Rabin at the White House on 16 March 1994, Clinton noted that the US would "maintain and enhance Israel's security as it continues to take real risks to achieve peace". This followed the framework established during their 1993 meeting in which Clinton told Rabin that he would minimize Israel's risks for peace and would provide economic and military aid to that end.
28. Speech by then Foreign Minister Yitzhak Shamir to the Knesset, 8 Sept. 1982. Quoted in Bernard Reich, *The United States and Israel: Influence in the Special Relationship*, New York, Praeger, 1984, p.217.
29. Abba Eban, interview published in *Jerusalem Post Supplement – Israel–U.S.*, 4 July 1984, page VII.
30. Vice President Al Gore, "US Middle East Policy: A New Era of Cooperation", 35th Annual AIPAC Policy Conference, Washington, DC, 13 March 1994.

The Effects of the Peace Process on the Israeli Economy

BEN-ZION ZILBERFARB

S INCE PEACE in the Middle East will undoubtedly entail significant economic implications for the region's countries, it is scarcely surprising that the ongoing peace talks have drawn considerable attention to the possible economic effects of the establishment of Palestinian autonomy in Gaza and the West Bank (GWB), in accordance with the September 1993 Declaration of Principles, and the signing of peace agreements between Israel and its Arab neighbours. Unfortunately, public statements about these effects are sometimes a mixture of hope and wishful thinking, sometimes a result of political attitudes towards the peace process, and at times a reflection of a parochial view of the process dictated by sectoral interests. This, in turn, has resulted in a series of conflicting and contradictory assessments.

The purpose of this analysis is to provide a balanced view of the possible implications of the peace process in general, and the establishment of Palestinian autonomy in the West Bank and Gaza in particular, for the Israeli economy, both in the short run and over the long term. To achieve this, the study is divided into two parts. The first assesses the direct effects of Palestinian autonomy on the Israeli economy, namely, those effects that are related to the economic ties between Israel and the West Bank and Gaza. The second part reports on the possible indirect effects – changes in the Israeli economy which are the result of the peace process, but are not linked to economic ties between Israel and Palestinian autonomy.

DIRECT EFFECTS

The economic ties between Israel and the new autonomy in the West Bank and Gaza are likely to affect the following four key sectors of the Israeli economy: trade, infrastructure, industry and agriculture.

Ben-Zion Zilberfarb is Professor of Economics and Dean of the Faculty of Social Sciences, Bar-Ilan University. Research for this analysis was done at the Azrieli Institute for Research on the Israeli Economy, Bar-Ilan University. The author would like to thank G. Feiler for helpful comments and G. Kurtzman for competent editing and typing.

Trade

Merchandise trade between Israel and GWB developed from $69 million in 1968 to $1,352 million in 1992, representing an annual growth rate of 13 per cent. As demonstrated by Tables 1 and 2, the Israeli market has been of supreme importance for the foreign trade of Gaza and the West Bank: about 90 per cent of GWB imports originate in Israel, and the Israeli market has captured an increasing part of GWB exports (85 per cent in 1992 compared to 43 per cent in 1968). Conversely, the share of the West Bank and Gaza in Israel's foreign trade has been small. In 1992, merchandise imports to Israel totalled $18.8 billion, a mere 1.3 per cent of which ($249 million) came from the West Bank and Gaza. Israeli exports in 1992 reached $13.1 billion, and about eight per cent went to GWB. Thus it is quite clear that the potential effects of the PLO–Israel agreement on trade between the two parties are far more significant for the West Bank and Gaza than for the Israeli economy. Nevertheless, some effects on the existing Israeli trade with GWB should be expected in the short run.

In order to evaluate the expected changes, one needs to know the rules that will govern trade between Israel and GWB in general, and the structure of indirect taxes and custom duties in GWB in particular. It is clear that if this structure is significantly different from the Israeli rates, then no open borders can be maintained as goods will flow freely from the less expensive economy to the more expensive one. Since, for political reasons, Israel objects to establishing any borders that may imply two sovereign states west of the Jordan river, it is assumed that indirect taxes and customs duties in Israel and GWB will be very similar.[1]

TABLE 1

MERCHANDISE IMPORTS OF GWB, BY MARKETS
(MILLIONS OF CURRENT SUS)

	Total	Share in total (percentage)		
		Israel	Jordan	Other Countries
1968	69.9	76.5	7.5	16.0
1975	406.9	91.2	1.3	7.5
1980	664.6	87.7	0.8	11.5
1987	1051.2	91.4	0.9	7.7
1992	1230.6	89.7	0.8	9.5

Source: Central Bureau of Statistics, *Statistical Abstracts of Israel*, 1993.

TABLE 2

MERCHANDISE EXPORTS OF GWB, BY MARKETS
(MILLIONS OF CURRENT SUS)

	Total	Share in Total (percentage)		
		Israel	Jordan	Other Countries
1968	35.5	43.1	43.7	13.2
1975	192.9	63.9	26.8	9.3
1980	345.2	65.6	31.1	3.3
1987	385.3	78.8	20.3	0.9
1992	291.4	85.4	12.9	1.7

Source: Central Bureau of Statistics, Statistical Abstracts of Israel, 1993.

Even with the same tax structure, trade is expected to be diverted from Israel to GWB. Under the current arrangement, imports to the West Bank and Gaza are handled by Israeli importers who sell the goods in those territories through local distributors. Once autonomy is established, there will be direct imports to GWB through local agents. This will result in a reduction of trade activity by Israeli importers. However, the effect on the Israeli economy will be very limited, since import activity adds to the Gross Domestic Product (GDP) only the value added of the imports (namely, the difference between the price in the domestic market and that paid to the foreign supplier).

Lower standards of living in the West Bank and Gaza and possibly lower direct taxes would enable the Palestinian importers to have lower profit margins. As a result, import goods may be cheaper to buy in the West Bank and Gaza. In addition to losing the GWB clientele, Israeli importers may lose some Israeli customers who will buy their goods in GWB. This may put some downward pressure on the profit margins of Israeli importers, to the benefit of Israeli customers.

In the light of these expected effects, it is not surprising that the Federation of Israeli Chambers of Commerce (FICC) recommended that the West Bank and Gaza be treated as part of Israel for the purpose of granting the status of sole agent importer. Moreover, their position is that Israeli standards and regulations regarding consumer service, spare parts, labelling and so on, would apply to all goods imported from GWB.[2]

Some support for the assessment that the effect of autonomy on trade between Israel and GWB would be small has recently come from a surprising source. A survey conducted by the FICC among its senior members reports that 61 per cent of the survey's participants think that autonomy would have only a minor effect on the Israeli economy.[3]

Infrastructure

The Palestinian economy requires a substantial investment in infrastructural projects: roads, electricity, ports and communications. As shown in Table 3, some $5 billion will have to be invested in infrastructure (excluding housing) over the long run (eight to ten years), while about $3 billion will be needed in the medium term (four to five years), implying an annual need of $750 million in infrastructural investment in the coming years. Financial resources will come mainly from foreign aid granted by the United Nations, the European Union, the United States and Japan. Israeli companies intend to take part in planned investment projects, and cooperation between Israeli and Palestinian companies would be beneficial to both parties. It would enable Israeli companies to enjoy economies of scale (lower costs resulting from a higher output with less than proportionate increase in inputs). To the Palestinian authorities it would save some of the essential investments in infrastructure, if they choose to use excess capacity of Israeli facilities.[4]

TABLE 3

PUBLIC SECTOR INVESTMENT NEEDS IN GWB
(US$ MILLION, CONSTANT 1993 PRICES)

	Total	Medium term	Long term
Water	480	280	200
Transport	500	250	250
Telecommunication	800	400	400
Electric Power[1]	2,200	1,100	1,100
Seaport	480	480	
Airport[2]	480	480	
Total	4,040	2,980	1,950

Notes:
1. Using Israeli facilities will reduce the cost by half.
2. This is an estimate for a new airport. If the Qalandia Airport in East Jerusalem is upgraded, the needed cost would be just $250 million.

Source: E. Sagi, Y. Sheinin, and M. Pearlman, "The Palestinian Economy and Its Link to the Israeli Economy", *Economic Quarterly*, New Series, No. 1, May 1983; The World Bank, *Developing the Occupied Territories – An Investment in Peace*, Washington, DC, Sept. 1993.

There are, however, three factors that may limit the future role of Israeli companies in GWB's investments:

(a) The Palestinian authorities would undoubtedly try to use investment projects as a major vehicle for providing jobs and incomes to

Palestinian residents. Consequently, high priority would be assigned to Palestinian companies and workers.

(b) For political reasons, the Palestinian authorities would make an effort to demonstrate "independence" from Israel by using their own companies or non-Israeli foreign companies. Many Arabs argue that Israel signed the agreement with the PLO in order to abolish the Arab boycott and to gain economic dominance in the region. Writing in this vein, the Egyptian newspaper *al-Ahram* argued that it would not be easy to establish regional cooperation with Israel because this would be used by the latter as a spearhead into the Arab world, and would force the Arabs to comply with Israel's wishes and end the Arab boycott; the boycott should therefore be kept as a drawing card until overall peace is established in the region.[5] The Saudi newspaper *Saudi Gazette* went a step further by arguing that Israel wished to utilize the peace process to control the Arab economies. Quoting Arab economists and bankers who met at a conference in Beirut, the newspaper argued that Israel would dictate economic conditions in the region because of its advanced industry and economy, compared to the Arab world.[6] To allay Arab fears of Israeli attempts to create a new "economic colonization" in the Middle East, Deputy Foreign Minister Yossi Beilin declared, at a recent conference held in Oman, that a common Middle East market should be put at the bottom of Israel's priority list.[7] Yet these fears and suspicions may lead, at least in the first period of autonomy, to the exclusion of Israeli companies from public contracts granted by the Palestinian authorities. Instead, preference may be given to Jordanian companies.

An example of the negative attitude towards cooperation with Israeli institutions was afforded in January 1994, when an offer by Haim Haberfeld, head of the Histadrut, Israel's trade union, to organize professional seminars for Palestinian leaders of trade unions was declined. In explaining this decline, Haidar Ibrahim, chairman of the federation of Palestinian trade unions stressed that the Palestinians had their own centres of training and seminars. It should be noted that the Histadrut organizes similar seminars for leaders of trade unions world-wide, mainly from the former Eastern bloc and developing countries in Asia and Africa.[8]

(c) Contributors of foreign aid would try, as part of their aid packages, to secure large projects to finance their own multinational companies.

It should be mentioned that some of the planned infrastructure projects make little economic sense. Specifically, the building of a port in Gaza, an airport on the West Bank, and an independent electricity system would require investments of about $2 billion over a four-year period. The bulk of this sum (up to $1.5 billion) could be saved if the Palestinians chose to use a more efficient and less costly way of using Israeli facilities, and gave up plans to build sea and airports. However, it is quite certain that, notwithstanding economic considerations, these projects would be carried out since they are viewed as national symbols.

Industry

It has been predicted by some Israeli economists that GWB will increase exports to Israel of cheap industrial goods aimed at low income groups in Israel in such areas as food, footwear and textiles.[9] Yet Israeli footwear and textile industries are already in the process of structural changes as a result of government policy on trade liberalization with Far Eastern countries. This in turn would mean that additional competition with GWB producers would have only a marginal effect, as GWB manufacturers of footwear and textiles would have to compete for their share of the Israeli market with cheap products manufactured in the Far East.

A recent survey conducted by the Israeli association of manufacturers among 370 of its members, lists two more sectors that are likely to be affected by autonomy – wood and its by-products, and building materials and quarrying. According to the survey, both these sectors are expected to lose more sales to GWB producers than the footwear and textile sectors; the estimated total damage to Israeli industry (measured in lost sales to GWB producers) is expected to be $1.5 billion over the next three years. At the same time, exports from Israel to GWB would increase by $700 million, so that the net effect of the autonomy would be a loss of $800 million in sales. However, as the survey report points out, these figures appear somewhat exaggerated, since they imply that industrial output in the West Bank and Gaza would more than double within three years. The report assumes, therefore, that the figures refer to a five-year span rather than three years. With this assumption, the expected net loss of sales for the Israeli industry would be about $160 million a year – less than half a per cent of its output.

A careful examination of the data suggests that even these figures are exaggerated. Merchandise exports from GWB to Israel stood at $250 million in 1992. Increasing exports to Israel by $1.5 billion over a five-year period implies more than an immediate doubling of GWB exports, which appears unlikely. A more reasonable optimistic assumption would be a 20 per cent annual increase in GWB exports to Israel, implying an increase of $1 billion over five years. This would represent a small net loss to the Israeli industry of $500 million in sales, about $100 million a year which is less than a quarter of a per cent of its output.

Nevertheless, the Israeli industrial lobby has expressed public concern over the possible damage to the industry as a result of the Israel–PLO agreement. According to a recent news report, the director-general of the Israeli manufacturers' association criticized the Israeli position in the Paris economic talks with the PLO for giving up the stipulation of Israeli standards on goods manufactured in GWB. He claimed this would lead to unfair competition between Israeli industry and imported cheap and low-quality products from the West Bank and Gaza.[10]

Finally, an interesting finding of the manufacturers' survey was that 85 per cent of its participants had expressed interest in cooperating with firms in GWB. The preferred way of cooperation was joint ventures, marketing agreements and sub-contracting of production to firms in GWB. Taking into account political constraints that would dominate economic factors, at least in the short run, sub-contracting would seem to be the most likely form of cooperation in coming years. This would also help alleviate the damage to Israeli firms caused by competition from GWB.

Agriculture

The agricultural sector plays a major role in the economy of the West Bank and Gaza. As can be seen from Table 4, the share of agriculture, forestry and fishing in the gross domestic product of GWB is 30–40 per cent. It is higher in the West Bank (up to 44 per cent in 1992) and lower in Gaza (about 25 per cent in recent years).

TABLE 4
SHARE OF AGRICULTURE, FORESTRY AND FISHING IN
PALESTINIAN GROSS DOMESTIC PRODUCT

	West Bank	Gaza	GWB
1968	37.3	31.0	35.2
1975	24.6	33.5	27.3
1980	31.9	24.0	29.8
1987	22.9	21.3	22.5
1992	44.0	25.5	39.5

Source: Central Bureau of Statistics, *Statistical Abstracts of Israel*, 1993.

In this respect, the Israeli economy is quite different as the share of the agricultural sector in its output is a mere 2.6 per cent. The decline in importance of the agricultural sector in Israel has been an ongoing trend, and it is likely that agricultural exports from GWB would increase. However, one has to take into account the powerful agricultural lobby in Israel, which would undoubtedly try to prevent the flow of agricultural produce from GWB. Indeed, the economic agreement between Israel and the PLO, signed in Paris on 29 April 1994, provides some protection to Israeli farmers. A free flow of agricultural goods between Israel and GWB would be permitted with the exception of six products: poultry, eggs, potatoes, tomatoes, cucumbers and melons. Restrictions on these products would be lifted in 1998. In response, the director of Israel's farmers' union warned that unless the economic agreement between Israel and the PLO was modified with respect to the agricultural sector, a "farmers' rebellion" would erupt.[11] A similar reaction came from the secretariats of the various settlement movements in Israel. However, despite these public statements, possible damage to Israeli farmers would seem to be low. Israel's Minister of Agriculture has recently demanded the provision of about $170 million in compensation to Israeli farmers over a five-year term. This would amount to about $35 million a year, or two per cent of the agricultural sector's output in Israel.

INDIRECT EFFECTS

The indirect effects of the "Gaza and Jericho First" agreement on the Israeli economy include those changes that are the result of the peace process, but not linked to economic ties between Israel and GWB. Unlike the direct effects, which would arguably be of limited importance, indirect effects may be significant and beneficial to the Israeli economy. Four areas are explored: trade between Israel and non-Arab parties, foreign direct investment, trade with the Arab states, and the potential "peace dividend".

Trade with Non-Arab Parties

The Arab boycott and tension in the Middle East has harmed Israel's trade relations with countries in the Arab and Muslim world, and with Third World countries which supported the Arab position in the Middle East dispute. The peace process nevertheless has enhanced Israel's political standing in the international arena, leading to the establishment of trade relations with countries that refused to do so prior to the Israeli–Palestinian accord. From the economic point of view, the most important new relations are those with the states of Central Asia and the Far East, such as India, Indonesia and Malaysia. The opening of the Far Eastern markets is particularly significant for exports of potash and phosphate from the Dead Sea.

Foreign Direct Investment

Multinational companies which hitherto have been reluctant to invest in Israel because of the Arab boycott, are currently exploring investment opportunities there. Bearing in mind that the level of foreign investment in successful developing countries is around three per cent of the GDP, the potential for foreign investment in Israel is very significant indeed, estimated at $2 billion per annum, compared with just $200 million in recent years.

Trade with Arab Countries

Another area that is often mentioned as a likely beneficiary of the peace process is regional trade between Israel and the Arab states. With the exception of Egypt, no direct trade exists today between Israel and other regional countries, but it is widely expected among politicians and businessmen that a comprehensive peace would generate a large volume of trade between Israel and the Arab world. Thus, for example, Israel's Foreign Minister Shimon Peres has already promoted the idea of a Middle East Common Market. But how realistic are these predictions?

An examination of past experience and existing trade patterns seems to refute the optimistic predictions regarding trade between Israel and the Arab states. First, these predictions call to mind similar assessments that followed the signing of the Israeli–Egyptian peace agreement in 1979. It had been estimated that the potential for trade diversion from Egypt to Israel was around $170 million (excluding oil), and from Israel to Egypt about $530 million.[12] The actual figures, however, represented a mere two per cent of this estimated potential: Israel exports to Egypt were just $5–7 million per annum in the 1980s and at the beginning of the 1990s, while Egyptian exports to Israel (excluding oil) were of a similar magnitude. This would hardly bode well for the prospects of trade between Israel and its neighbours.

Those who are optimistic about trade prospects, regardless of the Israeli–Egyptian experience, attribute the lack of substantial flows of trade between Israel and Egypt (apart from oil) to political constraints rather than to economic factors.[13] Yet, even if Egyptian–Israeli trade relations were ignored, there are two more compelling arguments that should make one cautious about the prospects for trade between Israel and its Arab neighbours. The first is that states in the Middle East trade very little among themselves: intra-regional trade accounts for only five to six per cent of total exports and imports. An explanation for this striking phenomena is that many countries in the region have followed import substitution policies. At the same time, oil states with capital surplus have had very open trade regimes which enabled them to import from anywhere in the world. The protected production of regional neighbours could not compete in terms of quality or price with world markets.[14]

Another factor explaining the low level of intra-regional trade in the Middle East is the composition of regional imports and exports. The former consist mainly of food, manufactures and capital goods, while the latter, in contrast, are dominated by primary goods, mainly oil. An assessment of the potential for trade between Israel and its neighbours should therefore take into account the dissimilarity in the trade structure of the trading partners. Recent estimates of trade similarity between Israel and some Arab states show that Israeli imports have little similarity with those states' exports. The level of similarity is just a quarter of that measured for Israeli imports from its major trading partners, such as Germany, the United Kingdom, France and the United States. Israeli exports, on the other hand, exhibit similarity to the Arab states' imports, which is close to that between Israel's exports and the imports of its major trading partners. However, taking into account political constraints that would limit, at least in the short run, the pace of trade development, the level of trade in the region, and the low level of economic development in the Arab countries, trade between Israel and its Arab neighbours is unlikely to exceed $400–$500 million annually.[15] This is a mere two per cent of the level of Israeli foreign trade and it is far from representing a major change in the region's trade structure, as envisaged by some politicians.

It should be mentioned that a 1993 report by the World Bank provided a more optimistic view of the trade potential between Israel and the Arab states. According to the report, the Israeli market would absorb 20 per cent of Egyptian exports, ten per cent of Syrian exports, and six per cent of Jordanian exports. Israeli exports would amount to only two per cent of imports of Egypt, Syria and Jordan. The basis for these estimates is a regression analysis of trade relations among countries outside the Middle East. It is questionable whether this relationship may be used as a forecast of Middle East trade structure which is quite different from other regions. Nevertheless, even the World Bank estimates of the additional annual trade between Israel and its Arab partners (about $1.3 billion) do not represent a major change in the region's trade volume – only a five per cent increase in Israel's foreign trade.[16]

The "Peace Dividend"

The most significant indirect effect of autonomy in the West Bank and Gaza on the Israeli economy is the long-term impact it would have on military expenditures. In the short run, the Israel–PLO agreement has put an additional burden on Israel's military expenditures. There are costs associated with the withdrawal from Gaza and parts of the West Bank, and with establishing new army posts and camps. The Israeli ministry of defence has already asked for an increase of about $200 million in its 1994 budget to cover these additional costs. However, the Israel–PLO agreement is expected to lead to peace agreements with the rest of the Arab world. Provided these peace treaties are signed and genuine peace prevails in the area, military expenditures may be cut in the long run. A recent study of the potential peace dividend assessed that, as a result of the cut in the size of the armed forces, skilled and highly qualified manpower would be diverted from the military to the private sector, thereby increasing productivity. The study also assumed a gradual ten-year reduction in military outlays, which would cut the share of military expenditures in the gross domestic product by half. The reduction in military expenditures was assumed to be diverted to an increase in investment. Under these assumptions, it was estimated that Israel would gain about $35 billion in additional output over a ten-year period. Real GDP per capita, which serves as a measure for the standard of living, would be 16 per cent higher ten years after the cut in military outlays than in a no-peace scenario.[17]

CONCLUSIONS

This study has examined the possible effects of the peace process on the Israeli economy. It has distinguished between direct effects that relate to the economic ties between Israel and Palestinian autonomy in the West Bank and Gaza, and indirect effects that are the result of the peace process but not related to economic ties between Israel and GWB. It has been demonstrated that, due to both economic factors and political constraints, direct effects of Palestinian–Israeli interaction in the areas of trade, infrastructure, industry and agriculture are likely to be quite limited.

Conversely, indirect effects on the Israeli economy are expected to be beneficial. Two areas of improvement would be the establishment of trade relations with extra-regional countries that refused to trade with Israel in the past, and the possible increase in foreign direct investment. Contrary to public statements by some politicians, trade between Israel and the neighbouring Arab states would be relatively limited. It may add around two per cent to Israel's foreign trade. Finally, if real peace and mutual trust prevails in the Middle East so that military expenditures could be cut, Israel would then be expected to gain some $35 billion in additional output over a ten-year period.

NOTES

1. Shortly before this analysis went to press, the economic talks between Israel and the PLO, held in Paris, were concluded. The general outcome is close to the scenario adopted here.

2. Federation of Israeli Chambers of Commerce, *The Effect of the Peace Agreement on the Israeli Economy*, D-9-2899, Sept. 1993.
3. See *Ha'aretz*, 4 May 1994.
4. For further discussion of the possible benefits of cooperation between Israel and GWB see E. Sagi, Y. Sheinin and M. Pearlman, "The Palestinian Economy and its Link to the Israeli Economy", *Economic Quarterly*, New Series, No. 1, May 1993.
5. *Al-Ahram*, 25 Nov. 1993, 3 Feb, 1994.
6. *Saudi Gazette*, 4 Jan. 1994.
7. *Yediot Acharonot*, 22 April 1994.
8. *Davar*, 14 Jan. 1993.
9. Sagi *et al.*, "The Palestinian Economy".
10. *Ma'ariv*, 28 April 1994.
11. See, for example, *Ma'ariv*, 28 April 1994.
12. R. Arad, S. Hirsch and A. Tovias, *The Economics of Peacemaking*, London, Macmillan, 1983.
13. H. Ben-Shahar, G. Fishelson and S. Hirsch, *Economic Cooperation and Middle East Peace*, London, Weidenfeld & Nicolson, 1989, Ch. 1.
14. S. Nemet, *Has Labour Migration Promoted Economic Integration in the Middle East?* World Bank, Middle East and North Africa Discussion Paper Series, No. 1, June 1992.
15. J. Silber and B. Zilberfarb, "Similarity in Foreign Trade Structure: the Potential for Trade Among Israel and the Arab Countries", Discussion Paper 94.02, The Azrieli Institute for Research on the Israeli Economy, Bar-Ilan University, April 1994. Also published in *The Economic Quarterly*, Summer 1994.
16. The World Bank, *Developing the Occupied Territories – an Investment in Peace*, Washington, DC, Sept. 1993.
17. B. Zilberfarb, "The Middle East Peace Dividend – How Large?" Discussion Paper 94.05, The Azrieli Institute for Research on the Israeli Economy, Bar-Ilan University, May 1994.

New Directions in Israel's Foreign Policy

AHARON KLIEMAN

S TRICTLY SPEAKING, until a definitive settlement of the Arab–Israel conflict is achieved, any references to Middle East "peace dividends" are unwarranted and premature, especially when the 1993 Oslo negotiating timetable has experienced serious delays. On the other hand, it is entirely appropriate that attention be called in mid-1994 to arguably the single most tangible peace *process* dividend thus far: the revitalization of Israeli foreign and overseas economic relations.

Nothing less than a far-reaching diplomatic revolution is currently under way in the critical realm of "Israel among the nations", marked by normalized relations with over 140 countries. Although incomplete (some 40 other countries still hold back on extending recognition), this reawakening of Israeli global statecraft has brought about a profound improvement in the political status of the Jewish state, while at the same time inspiring a new, proactive orientation at home to foreign policy-making. Should this recent momentum continue, the transformation will be thorough, with Israel having been converted from an international outcast to a member in good standing within the world community.

Popular impressions notwithstanding, this diplomatic renaissance did not happen overnight. Nor would it be fair to attribute Israel's new-found respectability to any single event or gesture such as the Rabin-Arafat handshake on the White House lawn in September 1993. As potentially important as the September 1993 accords may be, international rehabilitation has been a slow, prolonged and tedious process for Israel, dating back to the 1979 milestone peace treaty with Egypt, and gathering impetus along the way from both the 1991 Madrid peace conference and the opening of an official dialogue with the Palestine Liberation Organization (PLO) last year.

This political transformation is best mirrored through a larger

Aharon Klieman is Professor of International Relations and former Chairman of the Political Science Department, Tel-Aviv University, and is visiting professor (1994–95) at the University of Chicago's Middle East Center.

two-fold perspective. Even the briefest time-study suffices in contrasting Israel's regional and global position of late with what it was during the two previous decades. This favourable comparison is further confirmed by a revised, updated listing that shows graphically the sheer number as well as geographic range of countries maintaining formal ties with Jerusalem at present. Before proceeding to analyse the new direction it is taking, the following historical overview and statistical data help to reflect on how far Israeli foreign policy has come in recent years.

ISRAEL'S DIPLOMATIC MAP – THEN AND NOW

Precisely a decade ago, Israeli statesmanship suffered two major embarrassments. The first occurred in March 1984, when the Lebanese government of the day unilaterally abrogated the 17 May 1983 peace agreement that might otherwise have broadened the bilateral Israel–Egypt *rapprochement*. The second setback came on 14 December at the United Nations. An overwhelming majority of more than 140 countries endorsed four resolutions in a single day that, *inter alia*, declared that Israel "is not a peace-loving Member state" and called upon UN members to suspend economic, financial and technical assistance to and cooperation with Israel, and, in addition, to sever diplomatic, trade and cultural relations with it. For good measure, every government was advised "to cease forthwith, individually and collectively, all dealings with Israel in order totally to isolate it in all fields".[1]

These 1984 signposts of adversity in turn need to be seen as merely a continuation of the downward spiral already painfully evident throughout the previous 1967–75 period, in which a long string of Third World and Communist bloc countries unilaterally broke off ties in the wake of the 1967 and 1973 wars. Thus, the same UN General Assembly forum on 17 November 1974 voted 105 to four in favour of inviting the Palestine Liberation Organization to participate for the first time in the debate on the "Palestine question", as a prelude to PLO chairman Yasir Arafat's appearance at the rostrum from where he openly promulgated the liquidation of the "Zionist entity" and its replacement by a secular-democratic "Palestine".

Yet no single political tableau quite captures Israel's international ostracism and marks the absolute nadir in its external affairs than the blatantly anti-Israel resolutions adopted at the United Nations on 10 November 1975, defining Israel a racist regime in "occupied Palestine" while at the same moment equating Zionism with racism (72 for, 35 against and 32 abstentions). The effect was to deny Israel's *raison d'être* – its basic right to exist – while undermining the very moral, ideological and legal foundations of the state. Rising in response, ambassador Chaim Herzog bitterly denounced this "pernicious" and "wicked" resolution that is "for us no more than a piece of paper" (which he then proceeded to tear in pieces before the assembled delegations). Seeing the UN action as a shameful exhibition of how Israel was at once both envied and hated, he insisted that "on this issue, the world as represented in this hall has divided itself into good and bad, decent and evil, human and debased".[2] In Jerusalem the following day, Prime Minister Yitzhak Rabin described what transpired at the UN as an undisguised attempt "to place Israel beyond the pale" and "to impeach the essence and foundation of Israel".

Nevertheless, the negative effect of this campaign aimed at Israel's delegitimization is incalculable. Thereafter, and for the better part of the next two decades, the primary thrust of foreign relations concentrated on damage control. Diplomacy became essentially a defensive holding action aimed at averting complete isolation and total ostracism. Israeli emissaries, possessing fewer and fewer options, were forced into reliance upon less orthodox policy instruments like secret channels, clandestine anti-terrorist operations on foreign soil and illicit arms transfers in lieu of normal diplomatic conventions and government-to-government relations. Similarly, Israeli public opinion became increasingly hard-nosed and cynical towards the whole subject of pursuing relationships vis-à-vis the entire outside world, save the notable exception, to be sure, of special ties with the United States.

How markedly different is the diplomatic picture today, and the domestic mood as well. Both indicate a complete volte-face. Twenty years later, Yitzhak Rabin in his second term as premier operates within a markedly different external and internal environment. Not only has the erosion of Israel's legitimacy been arrested, but there is a dramatic upsurge in the number of new and also renewed contacts which in the aggregate amount to a sea-change in the general climate towards Israel.

The two-year period between the Madrid Conference in October 1991 and the Washington Accord in September 1993 saw 34 countries establish relations; another 13 followed suit by the end of the year and in the first three months of 1994 four more did likewise. The overall expansion of Israel's diplomatic map can easily be summarized: the number of active ties with other countries fell to an all-time low of 65 in late 1973, before inching upwards to 79 at the end of 1986; the number rose to 116 by August 1992, and to 138 in December 1993; as of March 1994 formal contacts stood at a high of 142.

Already indicative of what this might hold out for Israel, on 16 December 1991 a completely different correlation of political forces at the United Nations led to revocation of the infamous 1975 anti-Zionist resolution 3379; this time the voting was 111 in favour and 25 against, with 15 members abstaining. Likewise, whereas in the poisoned atmosphere of 1978 the 23rd session of the General Assembly could not even bring itself to laud the Camp David framework agreements as an encouraging contribution towards peace, on 14 December 1993 the 38th session cited the Oslo understandings as a positive step –and by a resounding majority 255 to 3 (Iran, Lebanon, Syria), with Libya abstaining.

Assuming the proportions of a groundswell, the most recent flurry of diplomatic exchanges with, and by, Israel leaves the roster of recalcitrant states largely limited to a hard core of Arab or Muslim countries unreconciled to Israel's existence, plus such anomalies as Castro's Cuba and North Korea. Yet even here there are noticeable cracks in the wall of resistance. For example, in February 1994 the Israeli chief rabbi was issued a visa to enter Cuba, where he met with Fidel Castro in Havana and with the local Jewish community. Meanwhile, reports persisted of secret contacts between Israeli envoys and North Korean officials.

Closer to home, the foreign minister of Qatar refused to be intimidated any longer by the Arab boycott of Israel. Early in 1994 he publicly boasted in Washington to meetings with Israeli cabinet members about a feasibility study for transporting liquified gas in tankers to Eilat, and from there by pipeline to the Mediterranean and on to Western Europe. Oman also quietly explored business links with Jerusalem, while a Persian Gulf diplomat was quoted as saying that "everyone in the region recognizes the strategic potential of ties with Israel".[3] Middle East *détente* scenarios gained further credence from the striking fact that five of the six Madrid multilateral working groups scheduled to reconvene in the spring of 1994 with the full participation of Israeli delegations were to be hosted by countries inside the region. Equally unprecedented, in March 1994 a delegation of Israeli Arabs received special permission to visit Syria, and President Asad himself granted them an audience. Forecasts went further, predicting closer, and possibly even official ties by the year's end with Arab states, mentioning Morocco and Tunisia as prime candidates. Providing the momentum generated by the interrelated Israeli diplomatic offensive and Arab–Israeli bargaining process can be sustained, it no longer seems far-fetched to entertain the notion of direct contacts with outlying Muslim countries like Bangladesh, Indonesia, Malaysia or Pakistan.

Clearly, incontrovertibly, the long international siege of Israel has been lifted, as a consequence of which the external political milieu is altered almost beyond recognition, whereby zones of vast potential opportunity replace zones of enmity and exclusion previously designated as off-limits to Israeli entrepreneurs, tourists or goodwill ambassadors. No less noteworthy, and equally as encouraging, is the improved domestic foreign-policy setting. It finds dual expression: (a) organizational, and (b) attitudinal.

CHANGE AT THE INSTITUTIONAL LEVEL

Almost from statehood diplomatic policy-making in Israel has suffered from a basic asymmetry of authority, power and influence between the ministry for foreign affairs and the ministry for defence. Although intended in 1948 as equivalent and complementary organizational actors, an increasingly sprawling defence establishment came to pre-dominate, with the foreign ministry in effect relegated to a secondary, often merely technical and supportive role. Among the principal causes: a compelling pro-security argument deriving from the embattled country's unrelieved security dilemma, almost unquestioned support from an Israeli public mobilized into a citizen army, a disproportionate share of national budget allocations assigned for meeting defence needs, and strong leadership at the top as personified by Ben-Gurion himself, Moshe Dayan, Ariel Sharon or Rabin. For our purposes, the point is that by losing the interdepartmental struggle the foreign ministry, during much of Israel's diplomatic career, was left with little or no say in key areas of foreign policy, extending from intelligence assessment and strategic planning to secret contacts or decisions governing weapons exports.

This, too, is changing. At present the ministry for foreign affairs has very much re-entered the bureaucratic fray, was instrumental in the 1990s worldwide diplomatic campaign and is playing an assertive role in the shaping of policy. What better proof than the Oslo break-through, which was inspired, directed and negotiated exclusively from within the Foreign Ministry, whereas this time the military authorities, including the Chief-of-Staff, were kept in the dark and outside the policy loop.

Several factors account for this reversal of bureaucratic fortunes. First and foremost, what Michael Brecher has referred to as the "high policy elite".[4] The team of Shimon Peres (Foreign Minister), Dr Yossi Beilin (Deputy Foreign Minister) and Uri Savir (Director-General of the Ministry) is quite unique in the annals of Israeli foreign policy for the combination of confident leadership, practical diplomatic experi-ence and hands-on, micro-management control over ministry activi-ties. Sharing a sense of where Israel as a society and state ought to be by the turn of the century, and convinced of the imperative need for peace with the Palestinians, they have carried out a restructuring of the foreign ministry meant to reflect its reordered priorities and to assist in putting Israel's best foot forward.

The reorganization plan, for example, features an enlarged policy planning staff along with a new human rights division and a department for promoting the peace process that bears responsibility for expanded Middle East regional programmes. The offices for cultural relations, for international organization and cooperation, and for overseas information services have each been elevated. So has the Ministry's "Mashav" division sponsorship for programmes which brought 2,415 people from 111 countries, including 20 that still do not have diplomatic relations – to Israel in 1993 on specialized training courses in agriculture, public health and other areas. In announcing his ministry's expanded agenda, Deputy Foreign Minister Beilin presented it as manifesting an Israel that feels more a part of the "community of nations", an Israel for whom "the world is important".[5] So important, and diverse, that it has required an increased budget and personnel in order to fill the dozens of diplomatic and consular slots necessitated by proliferating diplomatic ties.

Foreign ministry ascendancy has had one other attendant consequence in terms of how foreign relations are being conducted. There is evidence of a heightened awareness of the importance of (a) fundamental policy consensus, and (b) closer coordination on the formulation, implementation and review of policy, especially on the central issues of the peace process and relations with the United States. This is not meant to suggest the miraculous disappearance of the two traditional foreign policy hallmarks of divisiveness and partisan politics, merely that since 1992 in Israel, where everything is relative, one detects in the second Rabin government a greater degree of consultation at the top. Somewhat more thought is being given in the predecisional phase to alternative options and possible consequences; as well there is a marginal improvement in containing personality clashes and sharply divergent viewpoints that so often plagued Israeli diplomacy in the past. Whether this chronic weaknesses will recur, or not, as peace bargaining with the Arabs intensifies against the backdrop of both domestic and international pressures, remains to be seen in testing just how permanent are the internal improvements observable at the organizational and procedural level.

But what we have defined here as tantamount to a diplomatic revolution involves more than the way much of the international system now relates to Israel, or how foreign affairs are administered from Jerusalem and by its legations abroad.

CHANGE AT THE PSYCHOLOGICAL LEVEL

Being perceived of as an industrious, influential and involved country whose friendship and support are worth cultivating is also beginning to work its effect, in turn, on Israel's *Weltanschauung*, or (borrowing another social science term from Brecher), so-called attitudinal prism, through a positive feedback process. Each act of *rapprochement* – between Israel and individual sister-states, between Israel, and international agencies, between Israel, the media and world opinion – assumes symbolic importance, but also contributes to a deeper psychological healing process.

International respectability still takes some getting used to. The collective national memory summons up with perfect recall the general themes of pariahood – rejection, exclusion, isolation; so, too, do past grievances against particular unfriendly countries continue to rankle. These scars will not disappear easily. And yet, greater receptivity by outsiders cannot but help encourage a process of re-education at home, whereby the diplomatic arts long disparaged by generations of Israelis schooled in war start to take on a fresh appeal.

Broad segments of the Israeli public do indicate a non-ideological flexibility and willingness to revise their thinking and attitudes towards: (a) sharing confidence and trust with foreigners; (b) the efficacy of pursuing foreign relations; and (c) the larger historical-philosophical Jewish debate from the time of the biblical patriarchs through centuries of dispersion down to the present over the proper place of "Israel among the nations" and in a non-Jewish world.

One finds the first hesitant expressions of renewed confidence in Israel's ability to re-integrate itself into the family of nations, to extend useful humanitarian service whenever and wherever possible, and even to expect being commended for it. Surely the predisposition has always been there to be involved, to contribute and to be praised; Israelis as a rule are sensitive to the reactions of outsiders regardless of the *sabra* exterior facade projecting studied indifference and toughness. Obsessed by a perceived sense of encirclement by regional animosity, there has always been the need somehow to break out, to leap beyond the cordon of Arab hostility. As a country almost totally dependent upon the importation of strategic raw materials, Israel's leaders could never be other than alert to external developments; and goodness knows individual Israelis are compulsive tourists in addition to being avid consumers of everything foreign – from imported goods to ideas, fashions and cultural tastes in vogue elsewhere. Hence, they eagerly await full normalcy, and would welcome opportunities for unrestricted travel, economic integration, free trade and open door diplomacy.

Transforming Israel's world outlook goes further; indeed, to the very wellsprings of foreign policy. Scepticism towards the utility and worth of striped-trouser cocktail diplomacy is deeply ingrained in the collective Israeli psyche, again echoing past experience. None the less, under the impact of recent overseas gains resistance is lessening to the thesis that adept statecraft can contribute significantly to the national purpose. Similarly the argument for national security is being served no less by regularized diplomatic ties, subtle persuasion, patient negotiation, economic cooperation and just plain tact than through the use of force.

In fact, not since the early 1960s and the ambitious policy of foreign aid extended by Israel towards the emergent Afro-Asian countries have such voices of optimism been heard in public debate over world affairs as in the last year. Upon reflection, that earlier outreach programme represented the last hurrah, so to speak, of an idealistic internationalism inspired, on the one hand, by the old testament vision of the Jewish people as "a light unto the nations" and, on the other, by the sequence of four more contemporary diplomatic triumphs in the early days of statehood – UN endorsement for Jewish self-determination in 1947, speedy recognition by the Soviet and American superpowers in 1948, the 1949 Rhodes armistice agreements naturally but mistakenly assumed to be the first step on the path to peace and, also in 1949, the admission of Israel to the United Nations world body.

Subsequently, however, it was steadily downhill both for external relations and for the Israeli attitude towards them. By the time many of those same Third World recipients ruptured ties in 1967, Israelis had retreated into a protective shell. Their shared view of the world now came to embrace the polar opposite biblical image of Israel as a nation destined to dwell alone. Just as it was no longer politic or fashionable in the 1980s to speak of Zionism, *aliya*, socialism or *chaluziut* (pioneering), so did the "light unto the nations" theme of Israel in the vanguard position fall into disuse. The national debate was restricted really to only two schools of thought: one, the fore-mentioned pessimistic siege mentality positing in effect an isolationist stance; the other, a modest, almost minimalist approach towards Israel and the world. According to the latter, all that Israel should ask for is to be granted unexceptional status: a nation like any other, free of both special privileges and special censure, and deserving to be judged solely on the basis of its international behaviour.

One of the reasons why Israeli foreign policy is so interesting of late is because the debate about the preferred world view has not only presently been reopened and become more lively, but takes on a different flavour and nuance. As rarely before, Israeli opinion is clustered around all three alternative orientations. To be sure, an indeterminate number of people still cling to the minority hard-core view of Israel in a state of permanent war with the gentile world as much as with the Arab world. The main point, however, is precisely that this no longer represents the dominant prism for addressing the rest of the world. Rather, the largest majority of Israelis – especially among the younger, urban population – buoyed by the prospect of peace and its concomitant prize of full admission to the global forum, divide into two proximate camps: those whose optimism would settle for the normal status of a small state bent upon minding its own business; and those who literally for the first time in decades dare entertain the notion that, once given peace, the Jewish state might actually carry out the prophetic mission of marching in the front rank of the world's peacemakers.[6]

THE SHAPERS OF POLICY

The determining influence in security and foreign affairs is, as it has always been since the Ben-Gurion era, the role of personality. In the present instance, the trio of Yitzhak Rabin, Shimon Peres and Yossi Beilin share credit for steering Israeli diplomacy in a new direction, giving it greater definition and clarity than it has known for years.

Each of these political leaders has been individually instrumental, first, in breaking the familiar mould of Israel as an uncooperative, often renegade state actor, and, second, in replacing it with a more flattering image – pro-peace, regionally; proactive, internationally – that rests, moreover, upon a fairly broad domestic, public consensus. Most remarkable, however, is the degree of consensus among these three very different shapers of the new Israeli thinking, if not always on matters of tactics, then at least on the overarching strategy for getting Israel safely into the twenty-first century.

If we start with the premise that since Israeli government leaders are no different than anywhere else, a large percentage of what they say for local and international consumption might easily be discounted as self-serving, or as a mere lip-service. None the less, in trying to comprehend what is happening to Israeli foreign policy perceptions and policy positions, one is advised to pay closer heed to what these three top spokesmen have had to say on the subject in their public pronouncements. In this case words do matter, if only in shedding light on the respective motivations of Rabin, Peres and Beilin; but especially for underscoring divergent emphases even as they seemingly steer the country on an agreed course.

Shimon Peres

Of the three men, Shimon Peres from his recent writings and speeches comes across as clearly the most visionary and far-sighted. Admitting that "I have always tended to be overly optimistic", since his Oslo coup the Foreign Minister has made himself into the leading global enthusiast for a "new Middle East" (also the book title for his instant history and commentary on the peace breakthrough, rushed into print in 15 countries before the close of 1993).

Peres's blueprint for peace can be reduced to the following set of premises.[7] First, the world has been fundamentally altered and replaced by "a democratic, free, prosperous world that is changing and progressing, which, like a great river, sweeps away all obstacles in its path". This, in turn, compels Israelis "to replace our outdated concepts with an approach tailored to the new reality", in which such traditional security concepts as defensible borders, exclusive territorial possession and strategic depth are rendered obsolete in the face of missiles and other long-range offensive military technologies, and in which true power lies in science and economics rather than military might. "What is right for the rest of the world is right for Israel . . . [and] for the Arab nations as well", he writes. "The higher the standard of living rises, the lower the level of violence will fall."

Convinced that "without progress in solving the Palestinian problem, we will not resolve the Arab–Israeli conflict", Peres offers prescription for a "creative" and "optimal" solution: a political structure comprising a Jordanian–Palestinian confederation for political matters – since these two sides of the triangle "have no option but to coexist" – and a Jordanian–Palestinian–Israeli "Benelux" arrangement for economic affairs. Fulfilment of all these propositions – more in the nature of articles of faith than verifiable laws of probability – would ensure that "instead of visions of blood and tears, there will rise visions of happiness and beauty", at which point the first barriers will have been seen lifted between Israel and the goals so long eluding it of national security, regional integration and peace, and full international acceptance.

Yitzhak Rabin

That Shimon Peres and Yitzhak Rabin offer a study in contrasts is an accepted canon of Israeli politics, leaving experts to debate whether the cause is attributable to differences of biography and personality, or of political judgement and ambition. Where the more cosmopolitan Foreign Minister predictably tends to wax lyrical, and sounds almost messianic on his favourite theme of regional peace through economic developmentalism, Rabin, the taciturn former military Chief-of-Staff more given to introspection, is famous in Israel for his sober, deadpan and unemotional analyses of those short-term issues of direct immediacy and substance for Israel which alone preoccupy him. So, too, with the peace process inaugurated by the Rabin–Peres government in 1993. If the latter was led into the Oslo channel by the magnetic pull of a peaceful future Middle East, the former most likely was pushed into it by "worse-case" scenarios raising alarms about the imminent radicalization of Palestinian and Arab politics.

Yet precisely because of his known guarded lack of enthusiasm, and his reputation as "bitchonist" (security-conscious), Rabin's public statements are extremely instructive for the sense of openness and of internationalism they contribute to the debate inside Israel. Literally from the moment he reassumed office as Premier, Rabin has shown a high degree of sensitivity for the larger operational environment, and for Israel's ability to help modulate and fine-tune it. This was most pronounced on four prime-time public occasions, when Rabin addressed the theme of a new, healthier internationalist orientation in front of those five "constituencies" that inevitably make up Israel's diplomatic environment: at home, the Israeli electorate at-large, including the powerful defence complex; abroad, world Jewry, the Arabs, American and world opinion, as well as foreign governments.

In presenting his cabinet coalition to the Israeli parliament on 13 July 1991 (14 months to the day before the Oslo declaration), Premier-elect Rabin dutifully delivered a long and ceremonious statement of government policy guidelines which included a rather remarkable passage probably lost on most of the assembled Knesset members and the national television audience. In offering his assessment of global trends, Rabin stressed how in this closing decade of the century geographic atlases and history texts had been rendered obsolete by a progression of events: the crumbling of walls of hostility, the erasure of border demarcations, the collapse of both ideologies and great powers, the formation of new states alongside the demise of others and so on. This made it incumbent upon Israel to examine the opportunities as well as risks, and for him – "to do everything in his power to see to it that the country adapts to the changing face of international politics". He then sought to wean his listeners away from the twin pillars of conventional wisdom: that "the entire world is arrayed against us", and that as a consequence, Israel must resign itself to the fate of living apart. Uncharacteristically expansive, Rabin continued: "We have got to rescue ourselves from that pervading sense of isolation gripping us for the better part of a half-century. We must join the worldwide movement towards peace, conciliation and cooperation, for otherwise we shall be left behind, standing alone at the station platform."[8] Rabin pursued this line of thought in representing Israel at the fiftieth memorial ceremony commemorating the Warsaw ghetto uprising in April 1993. Here he sounded a seemingly dual yet coherent message. On the one hand, a note of toughness: "We are not here to forget or to grant forgiveness. Wherever we go, the memory of the Holocaust goes with us"; also, "the State of Israel is here to protect all Jews, and to serve as a place of refuge for Jews wherever they are".[9] But on the other hand, he ended his prepared speech by appealing for the highest Holocaust lesson: "No more violence, no more wars"; this after having opened with a line about how "we still believe that people and states can change".

The Prime Minister returned to the theme of foreign policy on

12 August 1993, when he told a gathering that "we are obligated to revise our thought processes, those embedded in us by years of enmity and hatred. We must think differently and see things differently, because a peaceful world demands a fresh set of concepts, definitions and teachings." Then, with the secret talks in Oslo unquestionably in mind, he emphasized: "This is the hour for change – to open outwards, to look around us, to dialogue, to fit in, to be forthcoming, to make peace."[10] What is singularly noteworthy, aside from the substance of his remarks, is the audience chosen for the occasion – the graduating officers of the national defence college and leading representatives of the influential military establishment traditionally known in Israel (very much like Rabin himself) for its innate conservatism, aversion to risk-taking and low regard for the niceties of global statecraft.

Nor did the key convert to peace diplomacy overlook the wider external audience in unveiling Jerusalem's new thinking. On 13 September, at the historic signing of the PLO agreement in Washington, Rabin proclaimed before the world media and a nodding President Clinton, as well as to the heads of the Arab states, the readiness of Israel to give peace a chance, "to begin a new reckoning in the relations between peoples" of the Middle East. Turning directly to the Palestinians, the veteran of Israel's wars and the chief architect of the 1967 victory made an emotional appeal: "We who have fought against you . . . we say to you today, in a loud and clear voice: enough of blood and tears. Enough."[11] His handshake with Arafat may have received by far the most extensive coverage, although in this instance Rabin's words are the more telling and indicative of the war-weary country's willingness – indeed, perhaps, eagerness – to follow its leaders on this less-explored course of peace through diplomacy and re-engagement with the world.

Yossi Beilin

There is good reason for assuming that future historians will credit Deputy Foreign Minister Yossi Beilin with being a prime mover in taking Israel on this new foreign policy course. For one thing, in terms of grand strategy, he was instrumental in opening and then pursuing the Oslo channel, in creating a "Palestinian option" and in arguing for a large-scale territorial compromise ultimately with the PLO. For another thing, in pragmatic terms, he was guided at each step of the way by a defined political philosophy,[12] somewhere between Rabin's incrementalism and concern with micro-detail, on the one hand, and the tendencies of Peres towards abstraction, on the other. Self-confident, often provocative and frequently outspoken, Dr Beilin shared parts of his operational code with an audience at Tel-Aviv University in February 1994, when he encouraged them to begin to visualize a different Israel enjoying the benefits of peace. Such an Israel, he professed, might then properly model itself after other small states such as Norway or Sweden in exercising a positive moral influence within the international system, otherwise incommensurate with its limited material resources.[13]

In operational terms, the youthful (46) Beilin exercised tremendous influence over the day-to-day functioning of overseas policy. Strategically positioned in the hierarchy of decision-making, he enjoyed considerable latitude in energetically wielding the staff and resources of the Foreign Ministry to promote his views on Israel and world affairs. Under his guidance, the Ministry's planning division drafted an unpublished 1994 position paper elaborating in somewhat more detail on Beilin's novel proposition. In the future Israel would seek as much as possible to participate in Middle East regional frameworks, to extend humanitarian and technical assistance to needy countries, to promote the cause of universal human rights, to join with other liberal societies in exporting democracy, to integrate itself in the working of the United Nations organization and its various commissions and agencies, and, in general, to do whatever it could in helping to ease international tensions. Conceivably this forward approach, with its keynote of active involvement, might well include assigning Israeli civilian, and even military personnel to global peacekeeping or peace enforcement missions. For all of the above reasons, despite being the junior of the three leaders, Beilin's assertiveness and input on recent policy-making should not be underestimated.

ENDS, WAYS AND MEANS

When the discussion moves from the plane of policy attitudes – the new outlook – to the specifics of both substance and style in contemporary Israeli diplomacy – its new look – the sense of transformation is definitely present and very real, although somewhat less dramatic and less pronounced. Which is to say that the diplomatic revolution, however genuine, does not extend to any fundamental redefinition of the national interest or wholesale replacement of the tools and instruments of statecraft. On the contrary, the pattern of continuity, albeit with shifting emphases, is about as dominant as that of discontinuity and change in each respective category of (a) policy objectives (the ends), and (b) policy techniques (the means).

The Foreign Policy Agenda

The declared aims of the Rabin government's foreign policy are hardly new or qualitatively different from any of its predecessors. The real distinction today, however, is to be found in the degree of earnestness towards achieving every one of the goals, and to the maximum. For now that the diplomatic floodgates have been reopened before Israel, it has become possible to contemplate as never before in the country's history the fulfillment in practice of the original set of foreign policy *desiderata* as adumbrated nearly 50 years ago by the Jewish state's founding fathers.

Nor is there anything terribly profound about stating these five or six vital 1990s' national interests. Reduced to essentials, they are: (1) legitimacy-recognition by, and normalized relations with all members of the international community; (2) Middle East peace – going far beyond "negative peace" – implying only non-belligerence – to an agreed, contractual settlement of the Arab–Israeli conflict, the exchange of ambassadors, genuine confidence-building and peaceful economic collaboration; (3) secure and recognized borders; (4) free trade, enabling the country's sustained industrialization through greater commercial integration within the global economy and ease of access to world markets. With these core objectives secured, Jerusalem would be in an excellent position to honour the two idiosyncratic, Jewish commitments of (5) affirming the self-image of the Jewish state and the entire Jewish people as a major positive influence in world affairs; while (6) enriching Jewish life and culture through closer contact with diaspora Jewry.

The goals have not varied, but the level of expectation about achieving them has. Under Peres and Beilin the Foreign Ministry has set its sights much higher; one senses a recommitment to actually reaching each of these objectives – and to the maximum: from furtive, back-door diplomacy to full recognition; not an armed truce with the neighbouring Arab states but normalization; open borders replacing barbed-wire fences; getting the Arab economic boycott lifted rather than making due with its circumvention; gaining praise for Israel's contribution to mankind instead of having to ask for the US veto as part of blocking efforts against UN resolutions roundly condemning Israel as a threat to peace; and, lastly, no longer settling for charitable contributions by fellow Jews but being able to advertise Israel – in the best teachings of Zionism – as a veritable rose-garden, dynamic society and prospective secure home for them and their families.

During this present chapter of Israeli foreign policy, diplomacy is not simply defined as a holding action. For the better part of four decades Israeli governments were forced, mostly by circumstances of threat, crisis and war into an essentially reactive, *status quo* posture. At least for now Israel is practising an activist approach, the signs of which are greater imagination and diplomatic initiatives, along with direct engagement in the Middle East and beyond. On behalf of the above-mentioned national interests Jerusalem has gone on the offensive, earning high marks overall for not only seizing opportunities when they might happen to arise, but for actually initiating them; creating openings rather than merely sitting back and waiting for them to happen.

If judged solely by this re-commitment to achieving in full the ambitious agenda of multiple and maximum interests, the resultant network of expanding bilateral and also multilateral connections is an undisguised blessing. Yet it becomes problematic in one sense, for it makes assigning priorities a necessity. Clearly, any small country with very limited resources would find it impossible to cultivate each and every one of its 140 and more affiliations with the same measure of intensity and dedication; certainly not in today's complex system of overlapping cross-cutting, competitive and upon occasion even mutually exclusive worldwide interrelationships. Given the jealous rivalry between Beijing and Taiwan, for example, how does Israel avoid alienating one or the other, or possibly both? Similarly, in the contest for Black Sea hegemony looming between Russia and the Ukraine, two countries where Israel has an equal interest in maintaining an open door. And, for that matter, what is the best course for Israel in the dilemma posed by objections from Washington to the independent feelers reportedly put out to such blacklisted regimes as Cuba, Iraq and North Korea?

Consequently, the Israeli diplomatic outreach programme increasingly resembles a delicate balancing act in consciously labouring to avoid any such compromising situations. Already the outlines are emerging that indicate a reshuffling of political priorities which begins with broad area concentration. For obvious reasons the United States and the North American trade area will continue to receive top billing. However, parallel with this mainstay of Israel's foreign policy, Jerusalem planners have introduced one significant innovation by re-targeting three promising geographic regions. After long neglect because of undue preoccupation with the US connection and the certainty that American friendship outweighed all other relationships, existing or potential – Europe, both east and west, has been rediscovered. Likewise, strategists are reawakening to the unlimited economic potential presented by the industrializing Far East, led by China and Japan. And for the first time the Middle East, as advocated by Shimon Peres, is seen as a realistic arena for interactions, extending northwards through Turkey to the former Soviet republics of central Asia.

This regional focus, in addition to encouraging greater diversification of effort, also lends itself as a useful ordering device for rationalizing and prioritizing policy preferences through targeting specific countries within each respective geographic subsystem. Through the careful assessment and projection of military, economic and political trends it should be possible to identify those rising local and regional powers with the most potential for influencing events in the first half of the next century; Germany in western Europe, Spain in the southern Mediterranean, Hungary in central Europe, Russia in Eurasia, Turkey in the Caucasus, India on the Indian subcontinent, Vietnam in Southeast Asia, Japan in the Pacific basin, Argentina and Brazil in the Americas, possibly Nigeria in black Africa, Morocco in the Maghreb, Iran or Iraq in the Persian Gulf and so on. Hopefully a policy of country specialization within regional and sub-regional frameworks might enable Israel to orchestrate a sustained diplomatic effort that is orderly, and which might secure many of these powerful local actors as strategic allies and also promising trading partners.

The Tools of Re-engagement

Turning next from the ends to the means of foreign policy, it might be asked, to what does the success of recent years owe? And in terms of the future, how best might Israel pursue this strategy of specialization with diversification? Here again, we find a case for continuity. The evidence does not indicate new or unfamiliar instruments of statecraft but only an enriched political and economic repertoire that is significant in itself. Short of being revolutionary, nevertheless, the feeling of a transformation in progress derives from a refinement in technique, different tactical and procedural emphases, and the particular mix of policy tools that is now favoured, and being employed to Israel's considerable advantage.

The defensive strategy adhered to from the late 1960s through the 1970s and the 1980s of waiting out Israel's many enemies was not terribly demanding; nor did it require any particular sophistication. Boiled down to its essentials, prudence required concentrating energies on fielding a credible military deterrent and (if that did not work) retaliatory capability. This mind-set viewed the UN and most of the outside world as alien, hostile arena best avoided; treated cultural and commercial exchanges as a poor substitute for political ties; and concluded information (*hasbara*) campaigns meant to win over world opinion were a waste of time, money and effort.

The 1990s provide a refreshing contrast, and draw out attention to several important modifications starting with the upgraded role of the Foreign Ministry, Home Office and of the professional diplomatic corps as themselves agents of policy implementation. Second are those changes taking place with regard to the salience of military transfers, of secrecy, and of the force option. Far more than can possibly be documented from the unclassified record alone, these favoured *modus operandi* significantly contributed to protecting Israel's core interests throughout the long diplomatic draught.[14] Instead of being jettisoned in this current phase of dialogue and normalization, all three tested policy tools can be counted on to maintain their importance in the ends–means calculus but will be subject to downgrading.

Arms diplomacy will continue as a fixture of external affairs, although probably in healthier proportion to other alternative instruments, especially non-military trade. Quiet diplomacy, too, logically becomes less critical in conditions of greater openness, yet retains a special place in those sensitive instances putting a premium upon discretion. Coercive diplomacy likewise becomes subject to redefinition: from offensive, cross-border interventions to a defensive mode of protecting Israel's borders.

Their downgrading, however, can also be explained by the simple fact that another set of complementary approaches and techniques is gaining respectability. Direct diplomacy, as its name connotes, marks reduced dependency upon the good offices of third party intermediaries like the United States or France to broker meetings or to represent Israel's interests with foreign governments that only yesterday refused to conduct face-to-face meetings. Multilateral diplomacy, symbolized by a redoubled presence at the headquarters of the United Nations, the European Union and various other international organizations in New York, Geneva, Strasbourg or Vienna, takes the direct approach a step forward, supplementing bi-national ties with participation in wider collaborative frameworks. Media diplomacy belatedly concedes the importance for Israel of sophisticated information and public relations campaigns in appealing above the heads of foreign leaders to the attentive publics, and to an amorphous yet influential world opinion. Cultural diplomacy in turn acknowledges the long-term contribution of people-to-people exchanges in building up friendly ties.[15]

However, pride of position in this augmented repertoire is now assigned to economic statecraft. Trade diplomacy might easily be mistaken for a mere extension of technology and weapons sales, since both share a search for foreign export markets, a strong economic motivation and the common belief that commerce translates indirectly into political influence as well. But economic foreign relations in a larger sense is far more suggestive of the deeper transformation discussed by this study, and of a more mature approach by Israel to international diplomacy. It recognizes how crucial commerce has become in modern foreign policy. It encourages an image of Israel as a normal country. And it exudes a sense of confidence in what Israel has to offer friendly countries by way of industrial trade, tourism, capital investment and joint development ventures. Trade statistics for the first three years of the 1990s already corroborate Israel's competitiveness. In many cases such as China, India, Japan, Turkey and the former Soviet republics and eastern European satellites, exports have doubled and even trebled with improved relations – thereby fostering the impression worldwide that it definitely pays to be on good terms with Jerusalem.

The image of Israel as something of an economic power benefits immeasurably from a final asset in this inventory of foreign policy tools, namely Jewish diplomacy and the so-called "Jewish connection". To some extent this may seem unexceptional, considering that Zionist statesmen since Herzl and Weizmann learned how to register political gains like the Balfour Declaration or the 1947 UN Resolution on behalf of Jewish statehood by converting the ostensible weakness of a people dispersed among the nations into an advantage. After statehood, later generations of Israeli leaders from Ben-Gurion through Golda Meir to Menachem Begin likewise could turn for moral support, as well as material assistance, to Jewish communities or perhaps to influential individual Jews in the common cause of assuring the survival and well-being of the Jewish state. In recent decades the contribution of the pro-Israel lobby in the United States readily comes to mind. The principal difference, however, is that this Jewish connection has been refined and orchestrated into something of a diplomatic art form.

In effect, Israel has taken the infamous and fraudulent "protocols of the elders of Zion" libel about the existence of an international Jewish conspiracy and turned it on its head. Whether exaggerated or not is irrelevant; the notion of solidarity and of resourcefulness in the Israel–diaspora relationship has taken hold, enjoying wide currency among foreign heads of state. It seems rather senseless, not to say impolitic, for Jerusalem to try to disabuse people of such inflated notions of undue Jewish worldwide political clout and financial influence, particularly as there is a good deal to gain, at least in an immediate and Machiavellian sense. Indeed, Israeli diplomats seem intent upon exploiting to their country's advantage this presumed ability to mobilize Jewish capital, business leaders, opinion-makers and power-brokers in the United States and elsewhere on behalf of overseas governments willing to improve relations with Israel. This winning formula has demonstrated its potency in any number of instances recently: Ankara's eagerness, like that of New Delhi's, to burden ties; the warm reception for Israeli emissaries and corporate executives in Russia and throughout the Commonwealth of Independent States (CIS); King Hassan of Morocco's public acknowledgement of long-standing contacts with top Israeli leaders; and fuelling the Palestinian peace process with pledges of future private Jewish development funding.

Still, Israel's resourcefulness should not be blown out of proportion. Nor should one lose sight of the basic asymmetry which lies at the heart of its foreign relations. Israel in effect matches the worldwide interests and ambitious goals of a great power with the resources and capabilities of a small state. Consequently, Israel is – and probably always will be –

in an unenviable geopolitical position: few carrots, and no sticks. In the context of normal, regularized diplomacy, not even a nuclear capability has within it the power to alter this disparity, so that on top of the other challenges before Israeli statesmanship there is this additional one of knowing how best to draw from the widest range of foreign policy instruments, while using each available lever of power and influence to the fullest.

FACING THE FUTURE

This inquiry might fittingly conclude on a positive note, describing Israel at peace with itself, with its Arab hinterland and with the global community at last. Yet precisely when, and because, the larger historical forces appear to be working in Israel's favour, presenting the contours for a "new Middle East" under the benevolent patronage of a "new world order", the nagging question nevertheless arises, but will this last?

Register it to compulsive Jewish anxiety (always tensed and waiting for the other shoe to fall) and to Jewish realism (Fukuyama and the millenarians notwithstanding, until the Messiah history never ends), compounded by residual Israeli insecurities; however, one is prompted to ask, just how solid are the foundations for Jerusalem's "new thinking" and orientation on foreign affairs?

Prudence, rooted in political realism, alerts us to the conditionality of foreign policy. In particular: (a) when Israel's hopes for reaching *el ha'menucha ve'hanachala* – for actually entering the gateway to the promised land of regional and international integration – are very much provisional upon the sister process of Arab–Israel peaceful conflict resolution; (b) when neither process is irreversible; and (c) when, for all the major strides taken along both parallel channels, the State of Israel and Israeli diplomacy are still far from any discernible finish line. This kind of limbo is succinctly captured in the heading of a newspaper article: "Powerful Israel? Or Endangered Israel?"[16]

Briefly, the answers to the questions posed here depend, as always, upon three key determinants: Middle East political developments, global crosscurrents and Israel's own sovereign acts of omission or commission.

Regarding the first, several endgames are possible in the Middle East peace process. One is that the Oslo framework talks experience arrested momentum (here the Hebron massacre in February 1994 is instructive), reach an impasse or suffer breakdown. Another outcome is that a final status accord with the Palestinians is hammered out and initialled, but either stops short of implementation or does not hold for long. Both eventualities would have negative consequences for Israeli overseas projects, especially should world opinion put the onus on Jerusalem for not being sufficiently forthcoming; in which case its current popularity will have proved short-lived. A third terminal bargaining outcome foresees a peace agreement that is carried out, perhaps securing for Israel the international respectability it wishes for itself; but a peace that is oversold at home and achieved at an extortionate price – far exceeding the Rabin government's initial negotiating principles of: no independent Palestinian state, a cessation of terrorism, close economic cooperation symbolized by early abrogation of the Arab boycott, a demilitarized West Bank and other security guarantees and so on.

Dogging Israel every step of the way along the piecemeal peace process is the ever-present risk of surprise originating from within the region. A leadership succession crisis or violent regime change in any one of the countries ringing Israel, an escalating conventional arms race or nuclearization of the Middle East, an inter-Arab hot war or any other sudden shift in the regional balance of power, the growth of Arab radicalism and the spread of Islamic fundamentalism – any one of these powerful destabilizing forces has the potential for derailing the process, thereby upsetting the Rabin–Peres–Beilin strategy and timetable for peace with normalcy.

Global realities and future trends make sweeping visions of permanent peace seem even more out of place. For Israeli diplomatists can hardly afford to be oblivious to the recrudescence of neo-fascism and anti-semitism across Europe, 50 years after the Holocaust, that threatens improved contacts with countries like Germany and Russia. Similarly, were Vatican diplomacy to press its traditional endorsement for internationalizing Jerusalem, the tensions still latent in the newly formalized relationship with the Holy See would set back ecumenicism. Nor are relations with the United States, the linchpin and pride of Israeli statecraft anywhere near being trouble-free.

In this survey of the diplomatic problems looming on the horizon, excessive reliance upon a single ally, the United States and the need to minimize contentious issues pose one special challenge. Another is the danger of entanglement in the affairs of too many allies. The network of spreading worldwide friendships includes warring or competing parties who, like Turkey in its struggle against the Kurdish PKK, pressure Israel to demonstrate solidarity by siding with it; the attendant effect will be to implicate and possibly even entrap Israel in local quarrels. Yet a third preoccupation in coming years will be *vis-à-vis* the Jewish world. There is a need for reordering the Israel-diaspora connection – which is the truly special relationship – in taking it from chequebook diplomacy to the magnitude of Jewish cultural diplomacy aimed at the strengthening of Jewish identity and the betterment of Jewish cultural and religious life both in and outside of Israel.

A final cautionary note perhaps to illustrate the highly conditional nature of Israeli foreign policy. Economic statecraft, with its encouragement of global development through peaceful competition and trade, seems like an exemplary strategy for Israel to push forward constructively on a number of fronts. Nevertheless, one is alerted to the twofold danger of excess in either direction. Half of the quandary is that should Israel succeed in its new-age economic policy, it exposes itself to the charge of meddling in other countries' domestic affairs and of being overbearing, thus offending national (and especially Palestinian and Arab) sensitivities; or, alternatively of being culpable for the failure of economic projects or for slow growth rates in developing countries.

The other half of the quandary, rather ironically, lies in the danger that having sold itself to foreign governments as not without influence in Washington, with Jewish corporate leaders around the globe and international banking circles, Israel will be unable – in a way of speaking – to deliver the goods. Inflated notions of Israeli political and economic clout have spread among otherwise worldly and sophisticated rulers. Surely the cordial reception given to emissaries from Jerusalem in world capitals from Ankara and Rabat, and from Madrid, Warsaw, Moscow or Tbilisi to New Delhi and Manila is explained to a great extent by this popular impression of Israel as instrumental – should it only be inclined to do so - in securing for them privileged access to Jewish businessmen in the US or elsewhere, and to the American media, the congress and possibly to the oval office of the White House in a unipolar world. This ploy stands to give Israel impressive gains in the short term. However, realistically it is quite impossible over the longer term for any Israeli government to satisfy such rising, and exaggerated, expectations.

Nevertheless, in the final analysis, such challenges and concerns should be seen – and even welcomed – as an inevitable, natural part of the diplomatic game of nations. Having to cope with uncertainty and complexity in a warring, dividing world is, after all, one of the distinguishing attributes of state sovereignty, and of sovereign policy that Zionist diplomacy petitioned for in 1948 as an antidote to 20 centuries of Jewish statelessness and political impotence. And in gearing up for the twenty-first century it is far better for Israel to face such foreign policy problems which, after all, derive from active re-engagement with the outside world than to have remained in the former, pre-1990s state of unsplendid isolation.

NOTES

1. General Assembly Resolution 39/146, "The Situation in the Middle East", in M. Medzini (ed.), *Israel's Foreign Relations: Selected Documents, 1984–1988*, Jerusalem, Ministry for Foreign Affairs, 1992, pp.72–8.

2. Full text of the three resolutions, "Invitation to the Palestine Liberation Organization to participate in the efforts for peace in the Middle East", "Question of Palestine" and "Elimination of all forms of racial discrimination" (Resolution 3379), pushed through on 10 November 1975 are in volume three of *Israel's Foreign Relations*, pp.349–52, as are the speeches of Ambassador Herzog and Premier Rabin.
3. Quoted in *The Jerusalem Report*, 24 Feb. 1994, p.27.
4. Michael Brecher, *The Foreign Policy System of Israel*, New Haven, CT, Yale University Press, 1972, especially Ch. 10.
5. *Jerusalem Post*, 27 Jan. 1994. *Mashav* figures do not include similar courses conducted abroad in 1993 for some 2,500 trainees in 25 countries.
6. Asher Arian, *Israeli Security and the Peace Process: Public Opinion in 1994*, Tel-Aviv, The Jaffee Centre for Strategic Studies, March 1994, JCSS Memorandum No.43.
7. Shimon Peres with Arye Naor, *The New Middle East*, New York, Henry Holt & Co., 1993. The following quotations are taken directly from the book.
8. "Divrei Ha'Knesset" (parliamentary proceedings), *Reshumot*, 13 July 1992.
9. Prime Minister Yitzhak Rabin's main memorial address, Warsaw, 19 April 1993. Courtesy of the Prime Minister's Office, Jerusalem.
10. Remarks made on 12 August 1993 at the national defence college, one month before the Oslo accords became public, and briefly reported by *Ha'aretz* the following day. The newspaper's editors belatedly acknowledged the speech's importance by reprinting the full text in the issue of 20 August.
11. *New York Times*, 14 Sept. 1993, p.12.
12. Beilin's thinking on future Israeli politics, society and foreign relations is set forth in his book, *Yisrael – Arbaim Plus (Israel – 40 Plus)*, Tel-Aviv, Yediot Acharonot Publishing House, 1993.
13. Transcript courtesy of the Jaffee Centre for Strategic Studies, Tel-Aviv University, which sponsored his lecture on 16 February 1994. His views were presaged by the ministry's director-general, Uri Savir, quoted by *Ha'aretz* on 19 January 1994 as counselling, "we have to adjust to being a contributor and not only a beneficiary".
14. Quiet diplomacy and arms diplomacy are dealt with in Aaron S. Klieman, *Israel & the World After 40 Years*, Washington, Pergamon-Brassey's, 1990. See also the author's *Israel's Global Reach: Arms Sales as Diplomacy*, Washington, DC, Pergamon Brassey's, 1985, and *Statecraft in the Dark: Israel's Practice of Quiet Diplomacy*, Boulder, CO, Westview Press, 1988.
15. One of the first to call attention to the likely importance of many of these techniques in international relations, rather ironically, was an Israeli, Abba Eban, in his book, *The New Diplomacy*, New York, Random House, 1983.
16. David Hoffman, "Powerful Israel? Or Endangered Israel?", *International Herald Tribune*, 21 Feb. 1994, pp.1, 4.

The Politics of Israeli–European Economic Relations

ROSEMARY HOLLIS

TRADE HAS become a politically loaded issue in relations between Israel and Western Europe. The European Union is Israel's largest trading partner, with Israeli imports double its exports to the Union. The imbalance represents a problem for Israel, especially since the Europeans are capable of using their economic weight to score political points. Since 1992, the creation of the single European market means that Israel must adapt to the challenges of competing in this new environment. Meanwhile, the prospect of a comprehensive Arab–Israeli peace agreement requires Israel to prepare for a new regional economic order in which Europe will play a central role.

On the face of it, peace between Israel and its Arab neighbours should open up new commercial possibilities and enable the integration of Israel into the rest of the Middle East, thereby reducing its reliance on Europe. In his vision of a new economic order for the region, in the event of peace, Israeli Foreign Minister Shimon Peres depicts a network of transnational highways and railways, interconnecting waterways and port facilities, and pipelines carrying oil and gas supplies from the Gulf to the Mediterranean. Peres also foresees the redistribution of resources across the Middle East, with shared energy and water systems, and a fund for economic development in poorer countries, from the Maghreb in the west to Yemen in the east, provided by donations from the oil producing states.

Yet, this idealistic scenario presupposes that resolution of the Arab–Israeli conflict can also remove all the other sources of conflict, rivalry and suspicion that divide people from their governments and states from each other in the Middle East. It also brushes aside the economic obstacles to greater regional integration. According to a World Bank report, inter-country trade in the Middle East accounts for only six per cent of the region's exports, which is one-tenth the amount of inter-country trade in the European Community.[1] There is little that the

Rosemary Hollis is Head of the Middle East Programme at the Royal United Services Institute for Defence Studies, London.

countries of the Middle East produce which their neighbours wish to buy. While it provides 25 per cent of world oil production, the Middle East consumes only five per cent of that total. Consumers prefer to buy manufactured goods from the West or the Far East, rather than purchase less competitive products from within the region.

Theoretically, as a more technologically advanced economy than its immediate Arab neighbours, Israel could be competitive in a regional market. Yet, fears have been voiced among the Arabs that Israel could acquire economic predominance to match its military pre-eminence. Israel's GNP of about $64 billion dwarfs Jordan's $4 billion economy and the Palestinians' $2 billion.[2] Meanwhile, Israel is at a comparative disadvantage to the Arabs in terms of relatively high labour costs. Vested interests in Israel, as in Arab countries, will seek protection against the unwelcome consequences of opening their borders to each other's products, and it is on such issues as these that Europe will have a decisive influence. As a provider of funds to underwrite Arab–Israeli peace moves, Europe will be more interested in ensuring balanced economic development from which all derive benefits, as a way to enhance stability, rather than a free for all.

The history of Europe's economic dealings with Israel has always been coloured by political considerations. Whereas the United States has developed a close political and strategic alliance with Israel over the past quarter century, cemented by US aid, Europe has adopted a more detached and critical stance, accompanied by increasingly explicit support for Palestinian rights. The most significant milestone in the evolution of the EC's policy on the Arab–Israeli conflict was the Venice Declaration of 1980, which identified a "special role" for Europe in the quest for peace.[3] Against this background, the EC has tailored its negotiating position on EC–Israeli trade relations to its appraisal of Arab–Israeli peace prospects.

During the 1980s, this meant that the EC insisted that Israel make provision for the Palestinians in the occupied territories to trade directly with Europe. In the initial run-up to the creation of the single market in Europe, the EC responded coolly to Israeli efforts to attain a new trade agreement with the Community. However, there was a significant shift in the EC's perspective after Israel and the Palestine Liberation Organization (PLO) reached accommodation on their joint Declaration of Principles (DOP), signed in Washington on 13 September 1993. Thereafter, the EC has taken the line that it can contribute most to future peace by funding Palestinian economic development and moving ahead positively on a new trade agreement with Israel.

Since the watershed of the Israeli–PLO agreement, two major strands in EC-Israeli relations have thus taken shape. First, the EC, or European Union (EU), as it has become politically, has agreed on the framework for a new economic partnership agreement with Israel, to supplant the 1975 Trade and Cooperation Agreement (TCA) and related protocols. Second, as a principal international donor pledged to under-writing the Israeli–PLO peace accord, Europe is set to become the largest single source of aid for the nascent Palestinian economy, with attendant implications for Israel.

Both Israel and the EU are interested in seeing that these two strands in their relationship are developed in a coordinated manner. In addition, through the vehicle of the multinational negotiations, instigated along with bilateral Arab–Israeli peace talks at Madrid in 1991, the EU has a role to play in Middle East regional development plans. This represents another factor in Israeli–European relations, influencing direct dealings between the two.

BILATERAL RELATIONS: THE HISTORICAL LEGACY

While the EU now takes precedence over its constituent member states in economic dealings with the rest of the world, those states retain importance as the formulators of EU policy. Consequently, Israel continues to lobby individual European governments as well as pro-moting its case with the bureaucracy in Brussels. In addition, Israel has special interests to pursue with each of the countries of Western Europe. Increasingly, however, it is difficult to disentangle those interests from regionwide concerns.

Relations with Germany are unique because of the legacy of the Holocaust and German efforts, including the provision of economic aid, to make some recompense for the past. In addition, Germany is the predominant financial force in the EU. Italy has led Europe in developing a formula for Mediterranean security and development. After years of estrangement, Israel and the Vatican were able to establish formal relations in 1993, in the wake of the Israeli–PLO peace deal. Spain, meanwhile, has importance for Israel partly as a competitor in European agricultural markets, partly as a potential bridge to developing relations with the Maghreb states. Yet, normalization of Israeli–Spanish relations did not take place until 1987, and in 1992 the Israeli president and Spanish monarch ceremonially laid to rest residual memories of the mass expulsion of Jews from the Spanish kingdom 500 years before.

Britain and France were critically important in the history of the modern Middle East, as the two imperial powers that drew up the map of the region after the First World War and the collapse of the Ottoman Empire. As the signatory of the Balfour Declaration in 1917, and League of Nations mandatory authority in Palestine between the world wars, Britain played a crucial role in allowing the development of a "national home for the Jewish people", which turned into the state of Israel when the British withdrew in 1948. The fact that the British tried to curtail the process they had initially endorsed, in the face of Arab objections and resistance, and turned away Jews aiming to escape to Palestine from persecution and death in Europe, left its mark on Israeli–British relations.

There was little love lost between the Israelis and the British when, for their separate purposes, they colluded, along with the French, in the 1956 invasion of Suez. So keen were Britain and France to conceal their collusion with Israel that they opted for a military strategy which was absurdly circuitous. In any case, it was the American intervention which decided the outcome of the Suez debacle – obliging Israel, Britain and France to withdraw – and set the seal on the demise of European imperialism in the Middle East.

After 1956 the decline in British and French influence in the region accelerated. Although, on the basis of their historical involvement, these two powers have been in the forefront of European policy-making on the Middle East and, as permanent members of the UN Security Council, Britain and France have a say in international pronouncements on the troubles of the area, particularly the Arab–Israeli conflict.

France was also to remain important for Israel as its primary source of arms supplies until the June 1967 Arab–Israeli War, when Paris embargoed arms sales to the protagonists. For the next 25 years, France refused to sell Israel any weaponry of any significance, until the mid-1990s, when a change of government in France heralded a policy shift. In March 1994 France and Israel signed a cooperation agreement on military technology and research, focusing specifically on lasers, drones and optronics.[4] Britain, meanwhile, was never a prominent supplier of arms to Israel and after the Israeli invasion of Lebanon in 1982, it imposed an embargo on military sales to Israel which was only lifted in spring 1994.

Among Israel's European admirers, sympathy for the little Jewish state in a hostile Arab neighbourhood more or less peaked with the 1967 War, when the Israeli forces took on Arab armies on all fronts and captured the Sinai Peninsula and the Gaza Strip from Egypt, the West Bank from Jordan and the Golan Heights from Syria. Israel's victory marked the beginning of a new phase in its foreign relations. By the time Egypt and Syria went to war with Israel in 1973, in an attempt to reverse their 1967 defeat, the United States had become the principal Western supporter of Israel. Britain and France, meanwhile, were already set on a course of giving precedence to their relations with the oil-producing states of the Gulf.

The Camp David Accords, which presaged the Egypt–Israel Peace

Treaty of 1979, were an entirely American accomplishment in which the Europeans played no part. To cement the peace, the US extended sizeable financial aid, both military and civil, to Israel and Egypt. Israel became the largest single recipient of US foreign assistance, with Egypt in second place. During the 1980s, US aid to Israel climbed to an average $3 bn per annum, about $1.8 bn of which in the form of military assistance.[5] The US also pledged to ensure that Israel would maintain a qualitative edge over the military capabilities of the Arab states, some of which, notably Syria, were firmly aligned in the Soviet camp. In Washington, meanwhile, the strength of the pro-Israeli lobby, especially in the Congress, became more pronounced.

WAKING UP TO A NEW ERA

The contrast between Israel's relations with the United States and its dealings with Western Europe was clearly apparent during the 1980s, as the Reagan administration made Israel a central component in its confrontation with the Soviet Union in the Middle East. This was also the period when the hard-line Likud Party gained ascendance in Israel and Jewish settlements in the occupied West Bank burgeoned. Any European involvement in Arab-Israeli peace moves was consistently shunned by the Israeli leadership. The best that Arab leaders could hope for from Europe, meanwhile, was that its governments might intercede with Washington on behalf of the Arab cause.

Not surprisingly, the US assumed far greater importance than Europe in Israeli foreign policy. Yet, the pointers to the future were there. Whereas Israel could look to the US for financial support in the form of aid, it was with Europe that its more significant trade relations lay. Also, as the European Community moved towards a more integrated internal market, the necessity for its external trading partners to pay attention to the implications of this trend became more pressing. The members of the EC signed the Single European Act in 1986, setting a target date of December 1992 for completion of preparations for a single market. Writing in 1989, Likud member (and future leader of the Party) Benjamin Netanyahu wrote: "Israel has always been so pressured by the rush of unpredictable events that it has found little time to prepare for the predictable ones. The 1992 economic union of the European Community is eminently predictable. It is an historic change, the preparation for which we can neglect only to our severe detriment."[6] According to an Israeli economic commentator, in 1989, Israel was ill-prepared on the commercial front for the impending changes:

> The Israeli economy is based on protection and everything that represents the absolute opposite of free competition. Only firms

that are capable of adapting to a competitive environment are able to develop export markets – many Israeli firms have shown that they can succeed handsomely abroad. Nevertheless, the domestic economy will be severely traumatised if it is opened up to foreign competition. That is why local manufacturers are fighting desperately to preserve their privileges and stall any moves in the direction of opening up.[7]

The *political* implications of the march towards European union also began to sound alarms in Israel as the 1980s drew to a close. According to Netanyahu, European governments could be expected to strive even more vigorously than before for a common position on international matters, and:

> Regarding the Middle East, those positions may not necessarily be always to our liking. It is no secret that in the past twenty years we have invested a major political effort in our relations with the US and not without significance. But it is also true that in that same period pro-Arab views have made headway among European opinion leaders. And it will not do to just brush aside the unfavourable voices. As Europe's political and economic clout grows, so will its stature in world affairs and its influence will be felt in the policies of other nations.[8]

The conclusion drawn by Netanyahu was that Israel must concentrate more of its energies on deepening and enhancing relations with European government leaders, broaden contacts with European parliamentary institutions, reach out to European journalists and public opinion, and strengthen ties to members of Europe's Jewish communities.

As it transpired, the creation of the single market in Europe was but one of a number of dramatic changes in the international environment to occur at the beginning of the 1990s. The chain of events began with the opening up of Eastern Europe and the fall of the Berlin Wall in late 1989, that signified the end of the cold war. Within a couple of years the Soviet Union itself had collapsed, leaving the United States as the only remaining superpower on the world stage. In the interim, the Middle East was caught up in the crisis triggered by Iraq's invasion of Kuwait. Then, in the aftermath of the 1991 Gulf War, the US took the initiative which led to the Madrid Conference and a new quest for a comprehensive Arab–Israeli peace.

Taking over as head of a new Labour and left wing government in Israel in June 1992, Yitzhak Rabin signalled his realization that the world had changed. In his opening address to the new Knesset, Rabin stated:

> We are no longer an isolated nation, and it is no longer true that the entire world is against us. We must rid ourselves of the feeling

of isolation that has afflicted us for almost fifty years. We must join the campaign of peace, reconciliation, and international co-operation that is currently engulfing the entire globe, lest we miss the train and be left alone at the station.[9]

Unlike its predecessor, the Rabin government was prepared to exchange land for peace with the Arabs. It also showed a new willingness to recruit European support for the peace process. However, there were still to be some stumbling blocks in the way of progress, and it was not until well over a year after the Labour election victory in Israel that the real breakthrough occurred, with the conclusion of the deal in Oslo between Israel and the PLO.

EUROPE AND THE ARAB–ISRAELI PEACE PROCESS

The cornerstone of the European Community's stance on the Arab–Israeli conflict was the 1980 Venice Declaration. This was important because it was issued in the wake of the Camp David peace accords brokered by the United States, and signalled Europe's willingness and intention to play a part in the search for a more comprehensive Middle East peace. The formulation of the declaration was also an achievement for the EC itself, as a milestone in its quest for a common foreign policy. From Israel's point of view, however, the Venice statement was most unwelcome, because it made explicit Europe's support for the Palestinian cause.

According to the wording of the Venice Declaration, "the traditional ties and common interests which link Europe to the Middle East oblige [the EC members] to play a special role" in the pursuit of regional peace. On the basis of UN Security Council Resolutions 242 and 338, passed in the wake of the Arab–Israeli wars of 1967 and 1973 respectively, as well as positions expressed by the EC on several occasions, the Venice Declaration stated that:

> the time has come to promote the recognition and implementation of the two principles universally accepted by the international community; the right to existence and to security of all the states in the region, including Israel, and justice for all the peoples, which implies the recognition of the legitimate rights of the Palestinian people.[10]

The Declaration went on to stipulate that the Palestinian problem was not simply one of refugees and that the Palestinian people must be placed in a position to "exercise fully their right to self-determination". It also said that the Palestinian people, and specifically the PLO, would have to be associated with the peace negotiations. Further, the EC stressed that "they will not accept any unilateral initiative designed to change the status of Jerusalem" and maintained that "settlements, as well as modifications in population and property in the occupied Arab territories, are illegal under international law".

Efforts by the EC to follow up the Declaration with active intervention proved half-hearted, however, and were stymied in any case by Israeli, Egyptian and US resistance and their preference for the Camp David process. Israel's opposition to the Venice Declaration was vociferous. In a statement issued on 15 June 1980, two days after the promulgation of the EC Declaration, the Israeli cabinet said:

> Nothing will remain of the Venice decision but a bitter memory. The decision calls on us and other nations to bring into the peace process that Arab SS which calls itself "the Palestine Liberation Organization" . . . all men of goodwill in Europe, all men who revere liberty, will see this document as another Munich-like capitulation to totalitarian blackmail and a spur to all those seeking to undermine the Camp David Accords and derail the peace process in the Middle East.[11]

Relations between Israel and the EC took a further knock with the second Likud election victory in Israel in June 1981 and, in the following year, the Israeli invasion of Lebanon. This was condemned by the EC, which called for the complete and prompt withdrawal of Israel's forces.[12] Following Israel's eventual pull-back to southern Lebanon, the EC was to continue to insist on a full Israeli withdrawal from the whole country.

On the Palestinian problem, meanwhile, the EC moved progressively towards more forthright endorsement of the Palestinian right to self-determination and the importance of involving the PLO in peace negotiations. In November 1988, the EC formally welcomed the decision of the Palestine National Council (PNC) to accept UN Security Council Resolutions 242 and 338 as the basis for an international conference, which implied, the EC concluded, "acceptance of the right of existence and of security of all the states of the region, including Israel".[13] The EC also expressed satisfaction at the PNC's renunciation of terrorism.

In all its pronouncements, the EC position ran counter to the course being pursued by Israel. The idea of an international conference did not appeal to the Israelis, since it would involve not only the US, but also other, less sympathetic, members of the UN Security Council. Also, Israel preferred the policy of dealing with the Arab states one at a time, not altogether. As for the PLO, before 1992 the Israeli government was implacably opposed to any dealings with the organization. For a time, it was even illegal for Israelis to have contact with PLO officials.

Consequently, Israeli peace moves concentrated on identifying alternative interlocutors for the Palestinians.

One such experiment occurred in 1987, when Shimon Peres, Israeli foreign minister at the time, reportedly reached a tentative agreement with King Hussein of Jordan, dubbed the "London Agreement" because that is where the secret deal was purportedly discussed. Although the framework agreement did feature an international conference, it called for negotiations thus initiated to be bilateral and it envisaged Palestinian participation under a Jordanian umbrella.[14] The scheme did not materialize, however, seemingly because leaks to the press on the Israeli side dashed its prospects before the Jordanians were ready to go public.

The next significant Israeli initiative was the plan floated by Rabin and Shamir jointly, during the Labour–Likud national unity government, in May 1989. This unilateral Israeli proposal was designed to build on the Camp David Accords and called for negotiations with Palestinians elected from among the inhabitants of the occupied territories, along with Egypt and Jordan if they agreed. Palestinian cooperation was not forthcoming, however, in part because of the exclusion of the PLO. Meanwhile, the Palestinian *intifada*, or uprising, which errupted in late 1987, persisted, bringing Israel much adverse publicity for confronting stone-throwing youngsters with armed soldiers.

During this period, Israeli leaders were bitter in their criticism of European support for Palestinian rights and the importance of the PLO. In January 1989, for example, Shamir told the chairman of the European Parliament, Lord Plumb, that it was difficult to conceive of the Europeans as participants in the political process in the Middle East, expressly because the EC had demonstrated a pro-Palestinian bias.[15] Rabin told a delegation of European parliamentarians not to teach the Israelis morals when it came to combating violence.[16] The French chairman of the European parliamentary delegates, meanwhile, told Knesset members in Jerusalem that the Europeans could not accept Israel's rejection of any European role in providing the auspices for peace talks, emphasizing that Europe is geographically closer to the Middle East than either of the superpowers and is Israel's largest trading partner.[17]

The pattern of Israeli–European disagreement on approaches to resolving the Palestinian problem persisted into the 1990–91 Gulf crisis. In the run-up to the coalition campaign to liberate Kuwait, the French considered meeting one of Iraq's demands half-way, by calling for an international conference on the Arab–Israeli conflict once Iraqi troops had evacuated Kuwait. However, the US was insistent that there should be no linkage between the two regional conflicts or implied rewards for Iraq. None the less, once the Gulf War was over, attention did turn anew to the Arab–Israeli confrontation, but the US overrode any alternative international moves and took the initative itself.

When the Madrid Conference was convened at the end of October 1991, the EC was not altogether satisfied with the role assigned to it, and Europe's cause was not helped by the fact that the Commission and the Chairman of the Council of Ministers had argued publicly about which of them should speak on the EC's behalf. In the event, Dutch Foreign Minister Max van der Broek, the serving Chairman, made a speech demonstrating the differences between Europe and the US. Van der Broek called specifically for Israel to accept the concept of exchanging land for peace and urged an end to settlement building in the occupied territories.

Keeping the EC out of the peace process was not a realistic option, whether or not the United States and Israel wanted it, since Europe was slated to pay much of the bill for regional economic development. Europe's central importance became clearer once the Oslo Accords set the agenda for practical measures to begin.

THE POLITICS OF TRADE RELATIONS

In early 1989, Israeli Prime Minister Yitzhak Shamir told a representative of the European Parliament that the EC should distinguish between the economic and the political aspects of its relations with Israel.[18] This has been a common theme in Israeli dealings with the EC, but since its agreement with the PLO, the Israelis have called specifically for Europe to compensate Israel in the economic sphere for steps it has taken on the political front. Politics and economics are basically too intertwined in European–Israeli relations to disentangle.

Europe's political leverage with Israel stems from the weight it carries in Israel's economic life. In 1993, 66 per cent of Israel's imports came from Western Europe.[19] Trade between Israel and the EC had steadily increased in value since the mid-1970s, with imports outstripping exports by a progressively larger margin, reaching 2:1 by the 1990s. As of 1993, the total volume of Israel–EC trade had exceeded $13 billion, with a deficit on the Israeli side of $4.5 billion.[20] Addressing a conference of the umbrella organization of Israeli high technology industries in January 1993, Israeli Prime Minster Yitzhak Rabin attacked the EC for discriminatory trade practices, saying: "In 1991, our purchases in Europe stood at $9 billion, and our sales stood at $4.5 billion. An addition of a mere billion in exports means 15,000 to 20,000 jobs. It is high time Europe changed its attitude, because Israel too has an option of buying elsewhere, and $9 billion a year is not a trifle to Europe either."[21] What Rabin wanted was a change in the terms of trade between Israel and the EC. In 1975 Israel signed a Trade and Cooperation Agreement (TCA) with the European Community, accompanied by a Financial Protocol, designed to further the aims and provide the means for implementing the TCA. This protocol was renewed subsequently, generally for periods of five years, with the last one to be agreed set to cover the period 1991–96. Since its formulation, other aspects of the TCA have been updated or extended with additional protocols, negotiated on an *ad hoc* basis.

By the 1990s, arrangements within the EC itself, as well as in Israel, had changed dramatically, compared to the 1970s, and rather than continue to update the existing trade agreement between them, Israel set about lobbying for a completely new deal. Of particular concern to Israel was improved access for its agricultural products, which have accounted for about one-third of its total exports to the EC. The accession of Spain and Portugal to membership of the Community, both of them competitors with Israel in the European market for citrus and other farm produce, has put Israeli exporters at an added disadvantage. Whereas the Iberian Peninsula states can transport their goods freely, by road, to other parts of the Community, Israeli products have to go by sea and be processed through EC customs.

Another complaint of the Israelis has been unfair trade practices within the community. According to one Israeli commentator:

> Most [EC] governments, despite directives to the contrary, shamelessly ensure that almost all contracts go to local firms, even if these are not the cheapest and most efficient. This can be done either through fixing the specifications required in favour of local products; or by rigging the tender procedures; or by not advertising tenders properly, or at all; or by simply refusing to accept bids from foreign suppliers.[22]

On the EC side, however, Israel has come in for criticism for not presenting an open market in return. The Israeli government purchasing law, giving preference to Israeli firms over foreign competitors, provided bids from the former are no more than 15 per cent higher than the alternatives, has been a case in point. At the same time, Israel's foreign currency controls have stood in the way of it meeting EC requirements for free trade in the financial services sector. None the less, since the advent of the Labour government in 1992, Israel has made progress in liberalizing its traditionally centrist economy and it would expect to dismantle more of its protectionist laws in return for new foreign trade agreements.

At no time, however, has Israel managed to persuade the EC to deal with free trade issues in isolation from political developments in the Middle East. In the 1980s, in fact, the EC deliberately used its economic weight to back its position on Palestinian rights. In 1986 the EC determined that the West Bank and Gaza Strip are "economic sectors not associated with Israel and Jordan", to which aid should be distributed directly and not through Israeli or Jordanian intermediaries.[23] In 1988, when the European Parliament was debating passage of three protocols on trade with Israel, it voted to deny final approval. By so doing, the Parliament signalled its rejection of conditions set by Israel for the implementation of an EC provision for Palestinian exporters from the occupied territories to deal directly with European buyers. The hold-up was temporary, but the point was made.

As Israel geared up to lobby for a new trade agreement with the EC, in the run-up to introduction of the single market, the European reaction was initially cool. In May 1992, Foreign Minister of the Likud government David Levy went to Brussels for talks with his twelve EC counterparts. At the same time as Levy made his visit, Brussels was hosting multilateral talks on economic cooperation in the Middle East. Israel had refused to attend those talks, in protest at the inclusion of Palestinians from outside the occupied territories. This displeased the EC and Levy found that he could not pursue his separate objective, because, as he was told by the EC ministers, Israel could not expect a reinforcement of its trade links with Europe while refusing to participate in EC-sponsored efforts to promote regional cooperation.

After the Labour election victory in June 1992, Shimon Peres, a noted Europhile, became Foreign Minister. His approach was to try to lobby on two counts simultaneously, on the one hand for European initiatives on Middle East regional development, and on the other hand for a new EC–Israeli trade agreement. In a tour of European capitals, Peres floated various ideas, such as a European-funded development bank for the Arab–Israeli sector of the Middle East, and desalination plants to relieve water shortages in the occupied territories. However, the Europeans reacted cautiously, foreseeing that any such moves would be politically sensitive in the absence of Israeli–Palestinian agreement on how to share economic decision-making powers between them.

On the issue of a new Israeli–EC trade agreement, Israel's Labour leadership also ran into some difficulties because the Europeans were angered by some of Rabin's measures to combat Palestinian violence, notably his decision in December 1992 to expel over 400 alleged HAMAS and Islamic Jihad activists to Lebanon. That move also held up the Arab–Israeli peace talks for over four months. In the meantime, Israeli and EC officials did meet for three rounds of discussions on upgrading the TCA, but progress was slow.

Giving vent to his impatience with the lack of progress, in July 1993, Prime Minister Rabin declared: "It angers me that Europe, which is a major market for Israel with which we have a $4 bn trade deficit, doesn't particularly help us, doesn't give us $3 bn in grants [and] hinders improving our trade balance for political considerations that have led them not to update the 1975 trade agreement."[24] The Prime Minister called on Israeli citizens to follow the government's lead and avoid buying products from companies that are not ready to make reciprocal purchases from Israeli firms.

Having signed the Declaration of Principles with the PLO in September 1993, the Israeli government redoubled its pressure on the EC. To give a final push to European consideration of the terms on which to negotiate a new trade agreement with Israel, Rabin went to Paris, Rome, Brussels, Bonn and London, while Peres put their case to Athens and had talks with his personal friend EC Commission President Jacques Delors. Before embarking on his tour, Rabin again sounded off at unfair discrimination by the EC and demanded to know, since EC differences with Israel in the past had been political, "what kind of disagreements can there be now?"[25]

In December 1993, the Foreign Affairs Council of the EU finally approved the Commission's draft mandate for negotiating a new trade agreement with Israel. The actual negotations began in February 1994 and were expected to take about six months to complete.

IMPETUS OF THE ISRAELI-PLO ACCORD

The Oslo Accords paved the way for Europe to take a central role in underwriting Arab-Israeli peace and in shaping a new regional economic order. Funds were immediately pledged to build up the Palestinian economy; the EC finalized arrangements for negotiating a new trade agreement with Israel; and multilateral talks on regional development, under European chairmanship, gained increased attention. The EC Commission set about achieving a balance between aiding the Palestinians and accommodating the Israelis. For their part, the Israelis saw a way, at last, to derive economic gains from political capital with the EU.

Israel aspires to a trade agreement with the EU that will give the Jewish state a status equivalent to that of EFTA (European Free Trade Association) countries included in the EU's so-called "common economic space".[26] Europe, however, has something less politically sensitive in mind. A partnership agreement specially designed for Israel would be acceptable to the EU, but since Israel is not a European country it does not qualify for an association with the EU akin to that of countries preparing ultimately to join the Union. European thinking on this is driven primarily by the need to preserve the special status of EFTA countries, like Switzerland, and also of the East European associate members of the EU, which are expected to apply for full membership in due course. However, by implication, the EU has clearly identified Israel as a Middle Eastern country, exterior to Europe and not entitled to a preferential political association with it.

In negotiating a new trade agreement with the EU, Israel has identified two broad objectives. First, on the purely technical side, the Israelis want a deal on agriculture, commerce, science, tourism and finance which takes into account the changes that have taken place in the EU on the one hand, and on the Israeli domestic front on the other. Second, they want an agreement that will reward and compensate Israel for the efforts it is making towards attaining peace with the Arabs.

On the technical side, Israel wants to ensure that it will not lose out to competition from countries like Morocco – which is to have its own partnership agreement with the EU – when selling goods such as agricultural produce to Europe. Israeli labour costs are much higher than those of the Maghreb states, and this is reflected in prices. Meantime, Israel wants Europe to acknowledge some of the sacrifices it expects to make in order to achieve peace with the Palestinians. For example, under the Washington Declaration of Principles, Israel is prepared to allow Palestinian agricultural products into its own market, which will incur the ire of the Israeli agricultural lobby.

Also, the 1993 accord envisages a redistribution of water resources between Israel and the Palestinians. To adapt to this, Israeli farmers will have to manage their crops differently. The EU could encourage this change by showing flexibility on quality regulations and seasonal import quotas for the products concerned, such as cut flowers. For its part, the EU is constrained by the demands of its own members, particularly those in southern Europe, for preferential treatment for their agricultural products. The most contentious elements in the negotiations for a new Israeli–EU agreement have been agricultural trade and rules of origin. One of Israel's long-standing demands, for special arrangements on science and technology, has made progress, however, in so far as these issues are to be covered by a new, separate protocol.

In Europe, Israeli calls for a deal to reflect progress in the peace process have not fallen on deaf ears, especially with the northern states with least at stake in the agricultural sector. Once the Declaration of Principles was signed in September 1993, President of the Council of Ministers at the time, Belgian Foreign Minister Willy Claes, informed Rabin that it would be a matter of honour for the EU to extend aid to both the Palestinians and the Israelis. Progress on a new Israeli–EC trade agreement would be speedy, Claes maintained, to "open our borders more to [Israeli] products and services and enhance cooperation in research and development" and "[T]hat way we will be supporting the peace process in a really pragmatic way".[27]

Yet given their track record on support for Palestinian rights, the Europeans are not going to lose sight of the purpose of compensating Israel for some of its undertakings for Palestinian self-rule. Immediately after the announcement of the Oslo Accords, the EU, already the foremost Western donor to the Palestinian community, pledged an additional 100 million ecu ($85 million) per year for five years. At an international donor conference convened by Washington in October 1993, arrangements were set in train for management and distribution of aid to the nascent Palestinian entity. While the World Bank will handle disbursement of the funds, Europe has a leading say in their allocation.

Europe's role in the provision and coordination of multilateral aid to the Palestinians dovetails with the EU's function in the multilateral peace talks. While only present as an observer in the multilaterals on arms control and security, the EU has acted as co-organizer of the talks on the environment, water and refugees. Most importantly, the EU is in charge of steering the multilaterals on regional economic development. In effect, Europe has an opportunity to boost the standing of the Palestinians *vis-à-vis* the other regional players in regional development plans which cannot go ahead until a comprehensive peace is in place. In the meantime, the Palestinian self-government that has come into being has needed immediate economic assistance.

Decisions made with respect to Palestinian needs could predetermine regional development options. For example, the Palestinians want their own port facilities on the Gaza coast. Technically, the Israeli deep-water port at Haifa is already capable of meeting the needs of both the Israelis and Palestinians, and it could also serve other countries, such as Jordan, if there were regional peace. However, in the near term, a separate port for the Palestinians would enhance their independence. Not surprisingly, the PLO leadership wants such a port to be built and the Israelis argue against it. Meanwhile, the Netherlands has come up with the financing for a consortium of Dutch, French and Italian contractors to build a floating harbour for Gaza.[28]

VISIONS AND REALITIES

Only Israel can make peace with the Arabs, but Europe is bound to have a say in the shape of the peace, by virtue of the EU's economic role in the process. As a vast, developed and now unified market, the EU is of fundamental importance to the economies of all the states in the Middle East and North Africa. In its turn, Europe has vital interests at stake in these areas, including energy supplies, investments and, not least, security.

Given their historical and commercial connections with North

Africa, the southern European countries are the most vulnerable to the effects of unrest on the other side of the Mediterranean. Yet with the creation of the European Union, the problems of one member are felt by all. Thus the EU has to juggle two political agendas in its dealings with the Middle East and North Africa: one is the competing priorities of its own members, the other is the diverse and interacting needs of the states outside.

These are the contexts in which Israel is viewed by the EU. By definition, this rules out the possibility that Israel can obtain an exclusive economic relationship with Europe in isolation from its regional surroundings. European support for the Palestinian cause is only one of the elements involved. The growth of Islamic radicalism is a more widespread phenomenon affecting European attitudes towards Middle East issues. Whether it suits Israel or not, the Europeans will insist on balancing their economic connections to the Jewish state with their dealings with the Arabs.

In the wake of the Israeli–PLO peace agreement, Israel has capitalized on European interest in underwriting the accord to promote its own case in Brussels. However, if the progress towards peace falters, Israel will have to fall back on unilateralist arguments. As it is, to compete in the European market, Israel must continue the process of adapting and liberalizing its own economy. Meanwhile, the internal politics of the EU stand in the way of Israel gaining more than a partnership agreement. An association with the EU equivalent to European countries in line for full membership of the Union is not open to Israel.

Israelis themselves may feel more affinity with Europe than with the Middle East. However, from the perspective of the EU, Israel is and will remain part of the Middle East. This raises the stakes for the peace process. It also points to the increasing importance of Europe, which used to be far less significant than the US, in the fortunes of Israel.

NOTES

1. David Makovsky, "Money Talks – Loudly But Secretly", *Jerusalem Post*, 29 Oct. 1993.
2. Abraham Rabinovich, "The Choice: Neo-colonialism or Integration", *Jerusalem Post*, 12 Nov. 1993.
3. Venice Declaration, *Bulletin of European Communities Commission*, No.6, 1980, p.7.
4. Robert Swan, "France and Israel: A Significant Visit", *Middle East International*, 18 March 1994, pp.8–9.
5. Institute of Jewish Affairs, *The United States-Israel Strategic Relationship in the Reagan Administration*, Research Report No.6, 1988, p.13.
6. Benjamin Netanyahu, "1992: The Political Dimension", *Jerusalem Post Special Report*, Sept. 1989, p.viii.
7. Pinhas Landau, "Just What is 1992 and Why Should Israel Care?", *Jerusalem Post Special Report*, Sept. 1989, p.iv.
8. Netanyahu, *1992: The Political Dimension*.
9. Address by Prime Minister Designate Yitzhak Rabin at the 13th Knesset, 13 July 1992,

Foreign Broadcast Information Service (FBIS), FBIS–NES–92-135, 14 July 1992, p.24.
10. *Bulletin of European Communities Commission*, No.6, 1980, p.7.
11. Israeli Cabinet Statement on 15 June 1980, *Survival*, Sept./Oct. 1980, pp.227–30.
12. Conclusions of the European Council, June 1982, in *Bulletin of the European Community*, No.6, 1982, p.16.
13. Declaration of the Twelve EC Member States, 21 Nov. 1988, in *PASSIA Diary 1994*, p.302.
14. Copy of so-called "London Document", as revealed by *Ma'ariv* on 1 January 1988, in *PASSIA Diary 1994*, p.302.
15. "Shamir Meets European Parliament's Lord Plumb", *Jerusalem Domestic Service*, 9 Jan. 1989, in *FBIS-NES-89-006*.
16. "Rabin Scolds European Delegates", IDF Radio, 10 Jan. 1989, in *FBIS-NES-89-007*.
17. "European Parliament Delegation Chairman on Talks", *Jerusalem Domestic Service*, 11 Jan. 1989, in *FBIS-NES-89-007*.
18. "Shamir Meets European Parliament's Lord Plumb".
19. Abraham Rabinovich, "Striving for a 'European Image'", *Jerusalem Post*, 29 Sept. 1993.
20. David Makovsky, "Rabin, Peres, Off to Europe to Talk Trade", *Jerusalem Post*, 23 Nov. 1993.
21. "Rabin Attacks EC for Alleged Trade Discrimination", Israeli Broadcasting Authority Television, in *BBC Survey of World Broadcasts (SWB)*, ME/1581, 8 Jan. 1993.
22. Landau, *Just What is 1992*.
23. "From Venice to Brussels – A European Position Reviewed", *al-Fajr*, 29 Oct. 1986.
24. Jose Rosenfeld, "Rabin Blasts Europe on FTA", *Jerusalem Post*, 8 July 1993.
25. David Makovsky, "Rabin Blasts EC for Trade Policies Towards Israel", *Jerusalem Post*, 9 Nov. 1993.
26. "Trade Talks with Europe to Open Next Week", *Jerusalem Post*, 18 Feb. 1994.
27. "EC Promises Israel a Better Trade Deal", *Jerusalem Post*, 2 Dec. 1993.
28. Rosemary Hollis, "UK Lags Behind in International Race to Help Build a New Palestinian Autonomy", *Guardian*, 16 March 1994.

Jewish Settlements in the West Bank: Past, Present and Future

ELISHA EFRAT

THE FUTURE of Israeli settlements in the West Bank is amongst the thorniest and most intractable problems confronting Israeli and Palestinian peace-makers, as they move to implement the September 1993 Declaration of Principles (DOP) and the follow-up May 1994 agreement. To successive Israeli governments, these settlements have been a legitimate act of enhancing national security and/or restoring Jewish presence in their ancestral homeland, so as to prevent part or all of these territories from returning to foreign hands. To Arabs and many international observers, the settlements have been a blatant violation of international law by an occupying power. The explosiveness of this perceptual gulf has been starkly demonstrated by numerous clashes between settlers and Palestinians over the years, most notably by the Hebron massacre of February 1994, which delayed the implementation of the DOP and raised fears over the continuation of the precarious peace process.

By way of assessing the future of Israeli settlements in the West Bank in the evolving peace process, this appraisal will trace the main stages of post-1967 Jewish settlement against the backdrop of the geographical, historical and political situation in the area, discuss the strengths and weaknesses of this national endeavour, and assess its resilience and viability.

BACKGROUND

Between 1949 and 1967 the West Bank was bounded by the armistice lines between Israel and Jordan, with no physical or economic links connecting it with the State of Israel. In 1947 there were 264 Arab villages in the West Bank, which had grown to 396 by the end of the Jordanian rule in 1967, a rise of 50 per cent. The increase in rural population during the same period was even more pronounced: from 283,600 to 598,500, or 111 per cent. This growth took place mainly in

Elisha Efrat is Professor of Geography at Tel-Aviv University.

the Hebron and the Jerusalem districts, rather than in the northern parts of the region, probably as a result of the internal migration of refugees and the settlement of nomads. It should also be noted that before 1947 there was a normal distribution of the population among the villages, only few of which numbered less than 500 or more than 3,000 inhabitants.

Arab agricultural settlement in the West Bank is a primary geographical phenomenon resulting from the physical nature of the region. The location of the villages, their distribution pattern, and the manner in which the physical conditions have been exploited to enable the inhabitants to sustain themselves and to preserve their way of life may be taken into consideration by all new settlers in this region, even if equipped with modern technologies. Most villages are located on the mountain crest, a plateau favourable for agriculture, and on soft terraces with relatively deep soil; they take advantage of the local topography, avoid main highways and do not encroach on agricultural land. The traditional Arab village in the Judean and Samarian hills demonstrates the role played by the climate frontier as a barrier to the extension of villages, and explains the concentration and sedentarization of the population at the edge of the desert.

The distribution of towns coincides generally with the watershed and follows the line of Hebron, Bethlehem, Ramallah, Nablus and Jenin. These towns constitute administrative, commercial, marketing and service centres for the surrounding villages, with Jerusalem having the additional function of being the regional capital.[1] All in all, traditional Palestinian settlement in the West Bank has been widespread and deep-rooted, and has occupied most of the cultivable land.

CHANGES IN THE SETTLEMENT MAP AFTER 1967

The sovereign territory of the State of Israel, as established by the 1949 armistice, amounted to 8,017 square miles. The occupation of the West Bank brought an additional 2,270 square miles under Israel's control, nearly a third of the country's territory. Prior to 1967, Israel's population stood at 2,750,000; following the Six Day War some 600,000 West Bankers, amounting to 22 per cent of Israel's population, came under occupation.[2] Twenty seven years later this ratio has remained almost unchanged: 5.2 million Israelis compared with about 1.2. million Palestinians in the West Bank.

The settlement map of today's Israel is fundamentally different from that of the 1950s and 1960s; it has been altered by the development of many additional new Jewish settlements in the West Bank, by the internal migration of population to them, and by new priorities of regional development. The 1970s and the 1980s were crucial in this

FIGURE 1

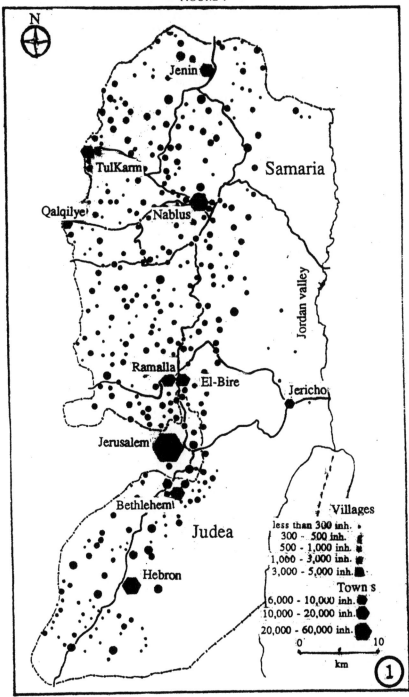

respect, for it was then that Israel's ties with the occupied territories were forged and a new map was effectively drawn, influenced by the new political reality created by the Six Day War.

Unlike earlier decades, settlement during the 1970s and the 1980s was largely predicated on political, rather than economic, considerations. Executed on a mass scale, rural and urban, public and private, in areas whose ultimate fate remains unknown, it involved penetration of a crowded Arab settlement fabric by a new type of settlement. This, in turn, has generated a regrettable diffusion of new settlements and has cast serious doubts on whether Israel's new frontiers will allow the maintenance of uni-national sovereignty and a democratic society.

THE ALLON PLAN

In 1967 the then Israeli Minister of Labour, Yigal Allon, presented the cabinet with a plan for the country's future borders, which proposed principles concerning peace arrangements with neighbouring states. The plan stipulated for a territorial compromise over the West Bank that would meet Israel's security requirements while taking into account the aspirations of the Arab population. It proposed to leave some 40 per cent of the area under Israel's sovereignty, with Israeli settlements along the Jordan valley serving as a security belt. Though never adopted as an official doctrine, the plan exerted a considerable impact on Israel's settlement map as long as Labour remained in power.

As early as 19 June 1967, less than a fortnight after the war, the Israeli cabinet decided to withdraw to the pre-war lines in the Sinai Peninsula and on the Golan Heights (with the exception of the Gaza Strip that was to remain in Israeli hands), in return for formal peace treaties and demilitarization of the evacuated areas. It was to change its mind, though, after the announcement of the famous three Nos – no negotiation, no recognition, and no peace with Israel – by an Arab summit in Khartum on 1 September 1967, and informed the United States of Israel's readiness to discuss essential matters with any Arab government.

To King Hussein of Jordan Israel offered a peace agreement but not on the basis of complete withdrawal. Shortly after the war it became evident that Israel was looking towards border modifications on the Jordanian front, as illustrated by the Knesset's incorporation of East Jerusalem into Israel on 27 June 1967. The significance of the Allon Plan, which was conveyed to the King in person by Allon and Foreign Minister Abba Eban, in two secret meetings in London during 1968, thus lay in its being the first comprehensive attempt to formulate a clear territorial stand regarding Israel's most problematic border, that with Jordan. The boundaries of the plan, derived from topographic and demographic considerations, were set between two longitudinal axes, one along the Jordan river, and the other along the eastern slopes of the Samarian hills; between them lay an arable and a rather sparsely populated area: the 1967 census showed no more than 15,000 inhabitants, 5,000 of them in Jericho. The envisaged width of the proposed settlement belt along the Jordan valley ranged between six to 15 miles, and a security strip was to join Israel's sovereign territory through a broad stretch of several miles along the Jerusalem–Jericho axis.[3]

The plan posited a large Jewish population in many settlements along the Jordan and the slopes of the Samarian hills, with agricultural settlements clustered around regional centres. The basis for this was the relative ecological advantage of the Jordan valley for early ripe winter crops and tropical fruits. The settlement of the Jordan valley was influenced by such factors as climate, the amount of water found locally, as well as the topographical features of the land (37,500 acres of land were found to be arable). Other key considerations were proximity to the Jordan river to secure the eastern border, as well as to the longitudinal road; maximum population of uninhabited areas; and avoidance of the occupation of land cultivated by Arabs.

In the run-up to the 1973 general elections the security rationale of the plan was underscored by Allon's fellow minister, Yisrael Galilee, who drafted an ideological platform for the Labour Party, supporting the concentration of "security settlements" along the borders and rejecting Israel's return to the pre-1967 borders and the establishment of a Palestinian state in the West Bank.

When conceived, the Allon Plan was a major innovation in Israeli strategic thinking. With the passage of time, however, it became outmoded. Rather than an asset, the concentration of settlements in a narrow strip of land came to be seen as a strategic liability that might restrict military manoeuvrability in the event of war; this scepticism regarding the utility of agricultural settlement as lines of defence in the occupied territories gained much ground after the October 1973 War, in which Israel was forced to hurriedly evacuate its settlements on the Golan Heights to prevent their seizure by the advancing Syrian army. Yet by 1994 Jewish presence along the Jordan valley had expanded to some 6,000 settlers in 30 settlements, compared with about 30,000 Palestinians who own 13,500 acres of land.

ENTER GUSH EMUNIM

Settlement activity in the West Bank has been carried out by Israel's two largest parties, Labour with its secular and socialist outlook, and Likud with its religious and nationalist stance. The former took a pragmatic approach to settlement, in line with Allon's concept of

FIGURE 2

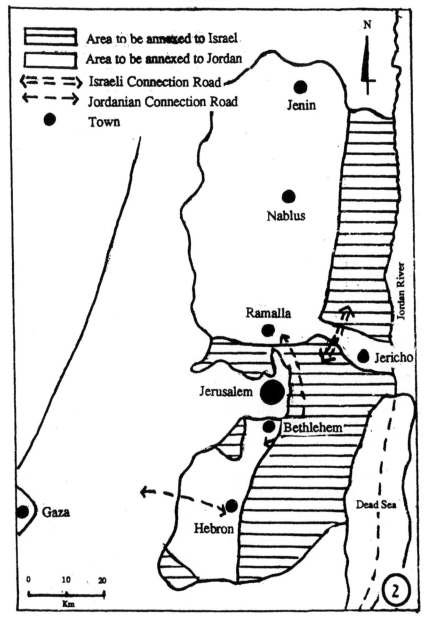

defensible borders, avoiding settlements in densely populated areas.[4] Likud, conversely, was committed to the territorial ideology of "Greater Israel" and insisted on the right of Jews to settle everywhere in the territories, not least near major Arab population centres. A new kind of pioneer Zionism thus emerged, one that exhorted Israelis to exercise their rights in their historic homeland and used nationalist and religious justifications to this end. These "new settlers" had to be highly motivated, since the regions in which they settled were densely populated by Palestinians, a thing that made their endeavour a rather hazardous one.

The ultimate manifestation of this "new settler" was provided by a new zealous movement established in 1974: Gush Emunim (meaning "Bloc of the Believers" or "Bloc of the Faithful"). Emerging at a low point in Israel's national morale, shortly after the traumatic 1973 War, this radical extra-parliamentary movement inscribed on its ideological flag the acceleration of settlement activity in the "Greater Land of Israel," Judea and Samaria in particular. The Gush's approach to the occupied territories was religious, indeed messianic. It was not only convinced of Jewish ancestral rights over Jerusalem, Hebron, Nablus, Bethlehem, Shiloh and their like; it believed in the sanctity of the Land of Israel and maintained that through settling in its historic homeland, the Jewish people, and not only Israel, was nearing its salvation.[5]

In practical terms, Gush Emunim aspired to settle the mountain crest and the areas of dense Arab population. This meant the creation of territorial continuity between the West Bank and the State of Israel. The movement invoked the pioneering spirit that had animated the Jewish people in the past, and was evidently encouraged by the tradition that had developed in Israel whereby settlers had never abandoned their land of their free will. Their first actions were to revive the Etzion Bloc, occupied by the Jordanian Legion during the 1948–49 War, and to reinstate Jews in Hebron, where they had lived for centuries, through the establishment of the suburb of Qiryat Arba. The growing influence of this young guard, mainly within the religious community but also among Likud supporters, led to the demand that the government annex the occupied territories to the State of Israel.

The Gush embarked on its settlement policy with a vengeance. Already in 1974 it established the settlement of Qeshet on the Golan Heights, and those of Ofra, Shiloh, and Kfar Kedumim in the West Bank. As the Labour government was unable to agree on what measures should be taken against Gush Emunim, not least due to the bitter personal rivalry between Prime Minister Yitzhak Rabin and Defence Minister Shimon Peres, the movement could pursue its activities virtually undisturbed. In 1976 there were 220 Gush Emunim settlers in the territories, and it was clear that the government would not remove them. They even prepared an ambitious settlement plan aimed at settling a million Jews in a hundred points in the course of one decade. The plan accorded priority to places along the Jerusalem–Nablus axis and two or three lateral axes traversing the mountain region. Its underlying principles were maximum spread of settlements; transfer of resources from the coastal plain to the hills; the establishment of a company to invest in industrial enterprise; rapid development of profitable projects; and state seizure of land whose ownership was unclear.

By 1977 Gush Emunim had already set up 12 settlements in the hills, comprising together some 500 acres of land. Each settlement consisted of a few inhabitants, employed outside the area and commuting to Jerusalem or the coastal plain; many settlers held on to their former dwellings as well. Likud's accession to power in May 1977 changed this modest beginning and gave the Gush a tremendous boost. Menachem Begin had never hidden his deep sympathy for this messianic extra-parliamentary group. He viewed Gush Emunim as a selfless pioneering movement and, as head of the largest opposition party in the mid-1970s, supported their settlement activities. Now, with Likud in power, Gush Emunim was being rapidly transformed from a small disruptive force on the sidelines of the Israeli political map into a mainstream movement.

Buoyed by its new prowess, in July 1978 the Gush prepared a second master plan for the settlement of 750,000 Israelis in the West Bank, the first 100,000 by 1981. The plan envisaged two central towns, Qiryat Arba and Ariel, each with a population of 60,000, and four smaller towns of about 20,000 people each; this, in addition to 20 10,000-strong urban centres and 25 concentrations of community settlements. Through this extensive network of settlements the Gush hoped to create an irreversible reality in the territories. Though it was obvious that such vast settlement activity would come at the expense of development in the Galilee and the Negev, and even on the Golan Heights, the Gush's grandiose plan effectively became the official policy of the World Zionist Organization and Israel's ministry of agriculture, headed by the maverick Ariel Sharon.

During Likud's first two years Gush Emunim succeeded in creating many facts on the ground, though the percentage of Jews of the total West Bank population remained practically nil. Government policy sought to break up the territorial continuity of the Palestinian population by means of the Jerusalem area settlements in the centre, those of the Jordan valley to the east, and of Gush Emunim at the heart of Samaria, in order to ensure that no autonomous entity above the level of local council would develop.

Gush Emunim created a new type of settlement, the community

settlement, suited to the hills, with their scarcity of land and water; each such settlement comprised a few dozen families and was based on private initiative and partial cooperation, with no obligation to work in the settlement itself; this also suited many of the residents who had no agricultural background. By 1980 there were 18 Gush Emunim settlements in the West Bank, and the decade witnessed an extensive settlement effort in the hill country. By the time Israelis went again to the ballots in 1981, the 7,000-strong Jewish population in the occupied territories had trebled. A decade later it exceeded the 100,000 mark.[6]

THE STRUGGLE FOR THE LAND

One of the basic channels of the struggle over settlement is land, both as territory and as a source of livelihood. Since the land potential is absolute, each party wishes to take possession of as much of it as possible. The Arabs cling to their land because it is ancestral, and because to them it means livelihood, happiness and honour. The Israelis, while sharing these basic aspirations, have hoped to detach the Arabs from their land as a practical means of settling in the area, for reasons of religious tradition, ideology, security and quality of life.

After the 1967 War an area of 1,445,000 acres of land came under Israel's jurisdiction. Only 30 per cent of the West Bank had been registered during British rule before 1947, mainly in the north of the Jerusalem–Jericho line. Where registration had been carried out, Israel could operate only on state land; this term covered virtually all categories of land, except that owned by local residents. Where no registration had taken place, and ownership was not recorded, the government adopted a land policy based on the Ottoman law, which designated empty land, mountains, rocky areas, and rough terrain, unknown to anyone and unused by any city or village dweller, as dead land; any person who needed such land could cultivate it, with official consent, but the sultan remained the absolute owner. The meaning of that law is that any land that is uncultivated or uncultivable, and is not recognized as private land, is state land. In view of the fact that 60 per cent of the land in the West Bank is not cultivable, and that a large proportion of it is unregistered, many areas could well be considered as state land. The Ottoman law allows exceptional rights on that land if a farmer has cultivated it for at least ten years. At the same time, the military government, with extensive powers regarding unregistered land, operated on the basis of national and security needs, which very often resulted in legal confrontation between local residents and the Israeli authorities.[7]

Between 1967 and 1977, the ruling Labour Party implemented the old ideology of the Labour movement, which, since the days of pre-

FIGURE 3

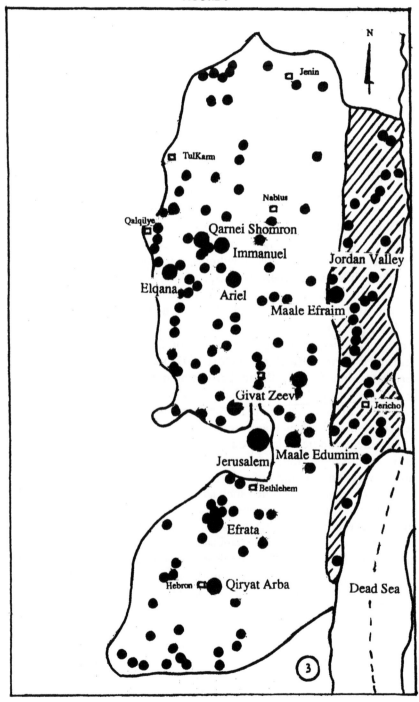

state had posited settlement on an agricultural basis. This ideology was also applied to the West Bank, which in turn necessitated the identification of fertile and arable land. By way of a solution, the government either declared the land as belonging to absentees and leased it to settlers, or seized it for security purposes. Likud's rise to power heralded a change in the concept of settlement across the "Green Line" (that is, the pre-June 1967 armistice lines) to one favouring settlement in all parts of the West Bank. In 1979 Israel's Supreme Court issued a ruling that confiscation for military purposes could not be used for the establishment of a permanent civilian settlement. This in turn pushed the government in the direction of the Ottoman law. Rocky areas and unused land were pinpointed through aerial photography and declared as state land. As two-thirds of the land were unregistered, and 60 per cent were defined as uncultivable, a great deal of land was available for urban settlements on a relatively small area, with no need for an agricultural hinterland. Most of Likud settlements were thus located on state land without impinging on privately-owned Arab land, and without expropriation for military needs.

To counter Jewish aspirations for control of the land in the West Bank, Palestinians resorted to a series of means. These included the unsupervised extension of village areas by scattered buildings; construction in isolated spots unconnected with villages; and resumption of cultivation of abandoned fields. They seized state land and established *faits accompli*, in the hope of arresting the steady diminution of land with every new Jewish settlement. These activities were especially obvious around Jerusalem and along arterial roads, and enjoyed political encouragement and financial support from the outside.

SETTLEMENT PLANS IN THE WEST BANK DURING THE LIKUD ERA

An noted earlier, an ambitious plan for the settlement of the West Bank, largely modelled on Gush Emunim's vision, was adopted in 1978 by the settlement department of the World Zionist Organization and Israel's ministry of agriculture. Its aims were twofold: to settle 100,000 Jews in the territories between 1982 and 1987, and to increase their numbers to half-a-million by the year 2010. The plan provided for the creation in the main of urban settlements in the vicinity of the Green Line, that would not be based on a hard core of ideological settlers, as had been the case in the past; rather, they would actually serve as residential suburbs of the Tel-Aviv agglomeration and Jerusalem, offering their Israeli residents a high standard of housing at a relatively low cost.

An extended version of the plan proposed the preparation of land for 165 settlements over a 30-year period, so as to accommodate up to a million Jews in the territories. Five towns of 10,000–30,000 families each were to be established, as were 36 suburbs, each with 3,000 families, 65 communities of 400 families each, and another 60 collective and small-holder settlements. The plan envisaged the construction of 5,000–6,000 units of dwelling per annum; the paving of 250 miles of roads; the expansion of existing rural and urban settlements; the development of industrial zones at the rate of 100–125 acres per annum, and continued acquisition of land. The areas identified for immediate implementation were Greater Jerusalem, the eastern slopes of the hills near Tulkarm, and south of Mount Hebron. The extended settlement plan did not concern itself with the empty areas east of the water divide, but aimed mainly at gaps between Palestinian villages on the eastern slopes. The model proposed was one settlement line to the east, loosely strung from north to south, and blocs of settlement to the west. The link between the blocs, and between Jewish settlements in the territories and pre-1967 Israel, would be maintained by a new infrastructure of local and national roads that would not be integrated into existing Arab roads and would allow for a settlement segregation.

To achieve these ambitious objectives, the plan divided the West Bank into three "demand zones" for residence and employment according to their distance from the metropolitan areas of Tel-Aviv and Jerusalem. Areas within 30 minutes' commuting time from these centres, or six to ten miles east of the "Green line", were defined as high-demand-zones; between 250,000 and 450,000 Israelis were envisaged to settle in these zones over a period of 30 years, or about 65 per cent of the total Jewish population in the West Bank. Areas within 50 minutes' commuting time to Tel-Aviv or Jerusalem were defined as medium-demand-zones, while territories further to the east were defined as low-demand-zones. The Jewish population in medium-demand-zones was expected to grow to 100,000–150,000 by the year 2010, while clusters or blocs of settlements in low-demand-zones were to accommodate between 40,000 and 70,000 Jews.[8]

CONCLUSIONS AND IMPLICATIONS

For all these grandiose visions and tireless toil, Israel's settlement ability in the occupied territories seems to be highly limited, both economically and demographically. The exorbitant investments in the territories have exhausted resources that could have otherwise been directed to development areas within the "Green Line". After 27 years of occupation, approximately 120,000 Jews live in the West Bank, as opposed to 1,050,000 Palestinians;[9] the gap between Jewish political and territorial aspirations and the actual reality thus remains very wide indeed, if not unbridgeable. Not least, the fact that a mere three per cent of Israel's Jewish population have settled in the territories affords a vivid illustration, if such were needed, of public reluctance to participate in this endeavour.

The Israeli–Palestinian Declaration of Principles of September 1993 has effectively brought the Jewish settlements in the occupied territories to their political and territorial end. Now they will have to play their last card following Israel's withdrawal from the territories and the establishment of a Palestinian autonomy, by ensuring some improvements for the future. In 1993 the Labour government froze further construction of houses in the settlements and prohibited the establishment of new ones; the settlers responded by adding infrastructure within the confines of their settlements and securing their commuting routes to "Green Line" areas. Yet as the bilateral negotiations between Israel and the PLO unfold, the feeling that they may not be able to stay in their places of residence indefinitely seems to be dawning on most settlers. Many houses in the settlements remain empty, as no Israelis would consider moving to the territories in these uncertain times. Even more indicative of the growing anxiety within the Jewish community in the territories is the formation of settlers' organizations with a view to negotiating a fair compensation in the event of evacuation. Last year's dramatic events, epitomized by the Washington accords and the ongoing bilateral peace talks between Israel and all of its Arab neighbours, have apparently invalidated the widespread assumption among politicians and scholars alike of the irreversibility of the settlement fabric in the West Bank. As the implementation of the first stage of the autonomy agreement in Gaza and Jericho approached, some Jewish settlers in these areas, having lost faith in Israel's political and military authorities, began barricading their settlements for the eventuality of Israeli withdrawal; this probably being their last desperate act before disappearing from the stage.

It may be safely assumed that in the future fewer and fewer roads will be protected by the Israel Defence Forces, so that the way of life in many settlements may be further restricted. Only clusters of settlements adjacent to the Tel-Aviv agglomeration or to Jerusalem will have a realistic chance to survive, while all the rest, mainly the remote and small settlements, will disappear over time. After all, even a quick glance at the West Bank settlement map would reveal that only in 21 Jewish settlements, out of a total of 128, does the population exceed the one thousand mark; another 26 settlements comprise 300–1,000 people, some 60 settlements – no more than 100–300 residents, while 12 include less than a hundred Jews; all the rest live in seven townlets. Put in a nutshell, 81 settlements, or 63.2 per cent of all Jewish settlements in the West Bank, have fewer than 300 residents, not a very comforting thought given the trials and tribulations that lie ahead.

The Jewish population in the West Bank has been too widely spread, in line with past government policy of large distribution of settlements so as to capture as much land as possible. Only a few urban or semi-urban concentrations of settlements in the region are likely to play a role in the future re-delineation of boundaries. Foremost among them are the townlets of Ariel, Immanuel, Elqana and Alfei Menashe, with their 30,000 inhabitants; the suburbs along the Beit Horon–Givat Zeev–Har Adar axis, with 9,000 residents; the townlet of Ma'ale Edomim, east to Jerusalem, with its 16,000 inhabitants, and the Etzion Bloc with its 8,000 settlers.

Undoubtedly the settlers will have to fight for their survival in a region increasingly governed by Palestinian autonomy. Some of them, those whose first homes in Israel are still available, will leave very soon. Others will leave when provided with alternative dwelling inside Israel itself, while a small group of extremists, the most ideological kernel among the settlers will remain under Palestinian rule and continue to claim the right of Jews to settle in all parts of Greater Israel. For how long these die-hard settlers will be able to last as a small island in a hostile ocean, and under what circumstances, remains to be seen.

NOTES

1. Daniel J. Elazar (ed.), *Judea, Samaria and Gaza: Views in the Present and Future*, Washington, DC, American Enterprise Institute for Public Policy Research, 1982.
2. W.W. Harris, *Taking Root: Israeli Settlement in the West Bank, Golan, Gaza and Sinai, 1967–1980*, New York, John Wiley & Sons, 1980.
3. Yigal Allon, "The Case for Defensible Borders", *Foreign Affairs*, Vol.55, No.1 (1976) pp.38–53.
4. It should be noted, however, that as Minister of Defence between 1967 and 1974, Moshe Dayan favoured urban Jewish settlement in the occupied territories, and defended the right of Jews to purchase land there. He envisaged the existence of two separate settlement complexes having economic relations. He did not claim Israeli sovereignty, but approved military supervision and control of places deemed vital for Israel's security.
5. On Gush Emunim's ideology and settlement activities see: Ehud Sprinzak, *The Ascendance of Israel's Radical Right*, New York, Oxford University Press, 1991; David Newman, "Jewish Settlement in the West Bank: The Role of Gush Emunim", Occasional Paper No.16, Centre of Middle Eastern Studies, University of Durham, 1982.
6. Geoffrey Aronson, *Creating Facts: Israel, Palestinians and the West Bank*, Washington, DC, 1984, pp.70–74; Meron Benvenisti, *The West Bank Data Base Project – 1987 Report: Demographic, Economic, Legal, Social and Political Development in the West Bank*, Jerusalem, Jerusalem Post, 1987.
7. Elisha Efrat, *Geography and Politics in Israel since 1967*, London, Frank Cass, 1988.
8. Benvenisti, *The West Bank Data Base Project – 1987 Report*.
9. These figure do not include Israeli residents in East Jerusalem.

Israeli Professionals and the Peace Process

MICHAEL KEREN

THE ANNOUNCEMENT of the Oslo Accords between Israel and the PLO at the end of August 1993 took many Israelis by surprise, but none more so than the intellectuals. Writers, scholars and journalists alike expressed "total surprise",[1] conceded "intellectual embarrassment",[2] admitted that the announcement struck them like a "thunder in August",[3] and defined it as a "strategic surprise",[4] a term normally reserved for the 1973 surprise attack.

This last analogy is particularly instructive. As in 1973, the intellectuals have yet again failed to foresee a critical development due to their entrenchment in an outdated conception, this time – the belief that conflicts are resolved as a result of cognitive changes, that is, changes in people's sensing and thinking. Israeli intellectuals have always conceived of peace as related to a change of heart and mind; peace will come once people "realize" the need to live in peace. Thus, when news of the Oslo Accords broke, much was written by intellectuals about the cognitive changes they involved and the consistency of these changes with their own writings in the past.

Writer Amos Oz, for example, argued that the accords proved that Israel and the Palestinians had finally recognized the need for coexistence. "Our moderate and pragmatic principle is being affirmed these days", he stated.[5] To writer Shulamit Hareven the accords signified a coalition between the "sane" elements among Israelis and Palestinians, while author Yizhar Smilanski defined them as a sign of maturity by people capable of abandoning their myths.[6] Similarly, intellectuals on the right castigated the accords as a value crisis. "Weariness, fatigue, normative emptiness are leading to the modern golden calf called, this time, peace", lamented Beni Katzover, an ideologue of the West Bank settlers, while writer Naomi Frankel viewed the accord as a pact with the devil, signed by "pragmatic politicians whose Jewish soul has degenerated".[7] Another writer,

Michael Keren is a Senior Lecturer at the Department of Political Science, Tel-Aviv University.

Aharon Amir, aspired for a different road to peace, one that ought to be "paved in the hearts and minds".[8]

That intellectuals emphasize the cognitive dimension in politics is not difficult to understand. As creators and disseminators of cognitive symbols their social status and political power depends on their capacity to convince others that these symbols make a difference. If peace in the Middle East depends on a fundamental change of attitudes, no less than on economic and political conditions, then it may be worthwhile to follow intellectual discourse and reward those participating in it. The truth, however, is that there was little cognitive change involved in the Oslo Accord; if anything, it was of the making of professionals rather than of intellectuals. This is why the intellectuals, thinking in cognitive terms, were taken by surprise, and why the debate between left and right over the accord sounds pathetic from a few months' perspective.

Both left- and right-wingers among the intellectuals correctly attributed the making of the accord to Israel's Foreign Minister Shimon Peres, considering it a "typical Peres-like operation".[9] But this "operation" had little to do with a significant change in the thinking of Peres, or for that matter - of anybody else who mattered, about the situation. As aptly noted by Palestinian scholar Azami Bashara of Bir-Zeit University, "Shimon Peres represents the interests and . . . ideology of a stratum of technocrats and managers, businessmen and industrialists."[10]

While Bashara carries his argument too far by attributing the professional stratum with colonialist motivations that can hardly be proven, it is arguable that the Oslo Accords were made by a knowledge–power nexus, dominated by Peres and his allies among Israel's professionals, who had little concern for cognitive changes. On the contrary, their main assumption was that no such changes were possible in the Middle East; hence the need to reach an agreement that would allow them to manage the conflict rather than to resolve it. In what follows, this appraisal examines the nature of that knowledge–power nexus and its approach to the peace process, in an attempt to shed light on the cultural presuppositions underlying the Israeli stance in that development.

PEACE AND THE PROFESSIONALS

The Oslo Accords consisted of a Declaration of Principles (DOP) on interim self-government arrangements, signed in Washington on 13 September 1993, and two accompanying letters of mutual recognition between Israel and the PLO. They would not have been achieved without the approval of Prime Minister Yitzhak Rabin, but their main architect was Foreign Minister Peres, whose fingerprints can be found in every clause of the DOP. With his deputy, Dr Yossi Beilin, he supervised the back-channel negotiations in Oslo which led to the accords, a fact that was by no means obvious. Approval of back-channel diplomacy was not in line with Peres's declared objection to negotiations with the PLO. Although the foreign minister seemed more moderate than politicians on the right, he was, in essence, a security "hawk", and it is hard to imagine that he underwent an instantaneous cognitive transformation into a "peacenick". To understand his role in the peace process, and the cultural presuppositions underlying it, one must look elsewhere – at Peres's long association with Israel's technocratic stratum.

Born in 1923, Shimon Peres was active since an early age in the *Ha'noar Ha'oved* youth movement which was affiliated with the workers' party – MAPAI. In 1940 he joined, as member of *Ha'noar Ha'oved* and its secretary general, Kibbutz Alumot in the lower Galilee. During the War of Independence he was asked by Israel's first Prime Minister and head of MAPAI, David Ben-Gurion, to undertake several tasks concerning weapons acquisition and manpower recruitment. After the war, Peres served for many years in the Ministry of Defence, becoming Director General in 1953, at the age of 29, and Deputy Minister of Defence in 1959 (when he also became Knesset member), a position he held until 1965.

With Ben-Gurion's secession from MAPAI in 1965, Peres joined him in forming the small RAFI party; four year later, as RAFI's secretary general, he led the move towards its re-unification with MAPAI and other parties to create the *Avoda* (or Labour) party in 1969. Since then Peres held various cabinet posts in Labour governments. After Likud's rise to power in 1977, he served as Labour's chairman and head of the opposition. In 1984 he became Prime Minister, heading the national unity government formed that year as a result of the political stalemate between Israel's two contending blocs: Labour and Likud. After 1986 he continued to serve, respectively, as Foreign and Finance Ministers in the national unity governments of the late 1980s; following Labour's victory in the 1992 general elections he became Foreign Minister in Yitzhak Rabin's government.[11]

Peres's technocratic roots go back a long way. During his tenure in the Ministry of Defence he played a major personal role in the development of military-related industries. Under his leadership, the Defence Ministry took over the armaments industry, expanded the aviation industry, and established electronics industries and the nuclear reactor in Dimona.[12] Peres formed close relations with defence establishments in foreign countries, especially in France, Germany, and the United States, and encouraged collaboration with them on defence-related research and development. In all these matters he worked closely with professionals, both within and outside the ministry. His office became a centre of major R&D endeavours; as a political figure he acted as champion of Israel's new technocratic stratum, namely, those professionals and their allies in the political system who share an interest in the modern technological state.[13] His writings and speeches called for industrialization, modernization, economic productivity, national planning, encouragement of higher education and extended use of science and technology. He went so far as to call upon the Zionist movement to focus its efforts to encourage *aliya* on the universities, rather than on the Jewish public at large: "Immigration to Israel should be from university to university and not from country to country."[14]

Professionals, often critical of the country's socialist leadership, could easily identify with Peres's call for a modern, technological Israel which reserved an important role for them. While many socialist leaders had an ambivalent attitude towards higher education, to Peres the university was "a laboratory for developing the economy, advancing the scientific potential and moulding the character of society".[15] At a time when Israeli educators still cherished agrarian values, Peres stressed the importance of industrial development, claiming that it was mainly industry, not agriculture, that demanded the individual's ingenuity, resourcefulness and vision. He used every opportunity to make appeals to those representing society's "both visible and hidden strengths", counting among them "good workers, outstanding scientists and technologists, resourceful, inspired investors".[16] It is scarcely surprising, thus, that an alliance between Peres and the country's professionals – scientists, engineers, economists, strategic analysts, public relations specialists, computer experts and the like – had emerged. He had always spoken a language familiar to that group, stressing the need to transform Israel into a society based on information, education and science-based industries.

When in 1984 Peres became Prime Minister in a national unity government, his alliance with the professionals deepened as a result of a common cause: the fight against the populist trends that had been intensifying in Israeli society since the early 1980s.[17] Hyper-inflation, an unsuccessful war in Lebanon, right-wing political rhetoric, and political stalemate between the two major political blocs, all raised the danger that politics be played in public squares rather than in regular governmental and parliamentary channels.

No one was more threatened by populism than Peres, who had been demonized by public-square demagoguery in the early 1980s. Moreover, his Labour Party depended on a structured polity that would allow it to control the distribution of resources through such institutions as the Federation of Labour (*Histadrut*) and the Sick Fund (*Kupat Holim*), and this institutional structure was being imperilled by populism. As Prime Minister, Peres ventured to fight populism by reducing inflation, taming extremist trends in foreign policy, and calming down tensions between social groups. To fulfil these tasks in a national unity government, in which political support by his own ministers was not assured, Peres mobilized the professionals. He formed a close circle of academically trained aides, worked closely with government-employed professionals, called scientists for consultations, founded both ongoing and *ad hoc* policy-making forums, held endless meetings with heads of universities and media organizations, and established a network of informal contacts between his office and academia.

The professionals were willing to lend a hand because, as professionals, they had a stake in an orderly political setting that would assure the free flow of information, so crucial to the professional's work.[18] To them, Israel of the 1980s seemed more of a backward country than the modern technological state they had a stake in. A condition of hyperinflation, domestic strife, lawlessness and isolation in the international scene marked to many the end of the Zionist endeavour. Zionism, the Jewish national movement, had always stressed the need to establish in Israel a model society based on the achievements of science and technology. Theodor Herzl, founder of the Zionist movement, had visualized Israel not only as a refuge to the Jewish people but as a haven: a modern, secular, well-functioning, creative and tolerant state in which the technocratic stratum would have a leading role.[19] The demise of Herzl's utopian vision for Israel became a common theme in Israeli writings of the 1980s.[20]

The populist trend had also a direct bearing on the social status of professionals. As social scientists Dan Horowitz and Moshe Lissak have shown,[21] populism, associated mainly with the economic policies and political rhetoric of Likud's leader Menachem Begin, Israel's Prime Minister between 1977 and 1983, impinged negatively upon the profesionals, as it tended to either disregard or ridicule certain components of their elite status such as education and cultural accomplishments. Moreover, sociologists, economists, social workers, medical doctors, Hebrew teachers, agriculture instructors and many other professionals who played an important role as mediators between the institutions of the Labour Party and their clients, were often ignored by Likud. For example, populist economic measures were taken in disregard of the advice by most of the country's economists.[22]

Peres, conversely, promised professionals a role in his model of Israel as a stable, well-functioning society, adhering to norms of the industrial world. Becoming part of the industrial world – the United States, Japan, and Western Europe – had been the ultimate goal for incumbents of this knowledge–power alliance. It was not uncommon for participants in meetings with Peres, in his capacities as Prime Minister, Foreign Minister or Finance Minister, to indulge in fantasies about rational, coherent, systemic, long-range, innovative processes of policy-making leading to the modern industrial society; "teams", "missions" and "task forces" were established in order to reform the "system". To the professionals in Peres's office the sky was the limit.[23]

THE ALLIANCE AND FOREIGN POLICY

Peres's moderate approach to foreign policy in the 1980s has often been explained by a cognitive transformation he apparently underwent; however, as claimed earlier in this article, it is safe to assume that no such transformation has ever occurred. Peres's moderation, expressed mainly in his advocacy of a territorial compromise with Jordan, was directly related to the nature of the technocratic milieu he was part of. That stratum does not of course share a unified political conviction, but its incumbents may be expected to have a stake in an environment that assures predictable rules of operation and the orderly flow of information without which they cannot function. Theoretically, the professionals may at times have an interest in war; in the 1980s they definitely had an interest in peace. Many of them were terrified by what they perceived as an unrealistic, aggressive foreign policy conducted by Likud, one that followed messianic yearnings and populist rhetoric. This was particularly apparent during the Lebanon War of 1982–85, launched by Begin's government in an attempt to form a new order in a neighbouring country, and conceived by many as part of an unrealistic, messianic attitude typical of populist regimes.[24]

Peres represented the opposite approach. As leader of the opposition during the Lebanon War, and later as Prime Minister and Foreign Minister, he advocated a foreign policy that closely adhered to the preferences of Israel's technocratic stratum: pragmatic, rather than messianic; moderate, rather than extreme; calculated, rather than capricious. Although critics considered his overtures to Jordan "a diplomatic house of cards",[25] especially because it involved a futile attempt to resolve the Arab–Israeli conflict without the participation of the PLO which represented most Palestinians at the time, he was the leader who made it possible for professionals to feel that peace was being advanced without shaking the territorial *status quo*.

A territorial compromise with Jordan meant essentially that while areas populated by Palestinians would not be administered by Israel, it would retain large parts of the West Bank in which professionals developed a stake, such as archaeologists conducting excavations, geographers leading sightseeing tours, hydrologists exploring water resources and, of course, architects, engineers and all other professionals who were engaged in the vast Jewish settlement effort there. Professionals' attitudes towards the occupation have never been systematically investigated, but the little involvement of professional associations in anti-occupation activities indicates that while many of their members were known to resent the biblical-messianic justification of the occupation, preferring security-related rationales, they had no reason to complain about it *qua* professionals. Many professionals fulfilled quite willingly the daily functions demanded by occupation, such as military and civilian governors, military judges, tax collectors, strategic analysts and so on. And while this caused certain ambivalent feelings,[26] with Peres in power these functionaries could feel they were serving an enlightened regime.

Peres also represented a deterministic approach to the Arab–Israeli conflict, which was consistent with the paradigm developed by regional experts, and which expected very few deeds by Israel to have a real effect on the hostility surrounding it. According to Dan Horowitz, two interrelated premises prevailed in Israeli security thinking: that Israel had no choice but to treat the Arab–Israeli conflict as a given, and that Israel was bound to take into consideration its narrow security margins, deriving from lack of geographic depth and demographic quantitative inferiority. He rightly cited Shimon Peres as a major subscriber to both premises.[27] Peres felt that Israel was involved in a confrontation that was unique in scope, in the varied assortment of Arab foes, the odds involved, and the condition of life constantly on the brink. In such a total confrontation, one's options were naturally limited.[28]

Peres's deterministic outlook was apparent in an article he published in *International Security* in 1978, where he argued that peace depended mainly on factors beyond Israel's control. Peres put his faith in the vague concept of a "proven dialectic" which should lead the Middle East from war to peace, suggesting that peace might be less dependent on the relations between Israel and the Arabs than on "developments that no one can stop, or prevent". He added that Israel must make "every possible effort towards peace, even if it takes us over unpaved roads [and demands] unusual solutions". These "unusual solutions" included such measures as building an Israeli–Jordanian common warning system along the Jordan River, which would not require fixing national borders, or forming an infrastructure for economic cooperation between Israel, Jordan and the West Bank which would supposedly prevent conflict over the boundaries of these three territorial entities.[29]

The article thus contains the seeds of the approach that would guide Peres and the professionals in their future activities regarding the Arab–Israeli conflict. The deterministic view of the conflict and the scepticism regarding its resolvability have led them to opt for pragmatic fixes, namely, solutions that do not necessarily go to the core of the conflict but rather aim at its management; instead of searching for a breakthrough in the conflict, technological devices, intermediate solutions and complex arrangements are sought. This is where professionals play a major role. Instead of diplomats designing models of peace and ways to reach them, professionals devise autonomies, federations, open bridges, good fences, mutual warning systems, and the like.[30]

This was exactly the approach which lay behind the Oslo Accords. In the 1990s the partner has changed; the Jordanian option had been exhausted and it was clear to Peres, as it was to Rabin, that the PLO, economically and politically weakened in the wake of the the 1991 Gulf War, would be the natural partner for an agreement. But the drama concerning the apparent reconciliation between Israel and the Palestinian people, played out on the south lawn of the White House on 13 September 1993, has been quite exaggerated. What Avi Shlaim labelled as "the mother of all breakthroughs"[31] did not involve a cognitive change; from the Israeli perspective, the Declaration of Principles could be considered an outgrowth of the pragmatic trait represented by Israel's technocratic stratum, of seeking "fixes" to the Arab–Israeli conflict.

THE CULTURAL PRESUPPOSITIONS OF THE DECLARATION OF PRINCIPLES

The nature of a "fix" is that it does not solve a problem but diverts it to a different court. Rather than play the game by its own rules, engage in the tribal wars of the Middle East or find ways to peacefully integrate in the region's social, economic and political order, "fixers" seek to make the game a manageable one by using professional knowledge as a means to break the constraints imposed by fundamental differences between people. This cultural trait may be labelled as "the Dimona syndrome" after the greatest "fix" associated with Peres's career – the construction of a nuclear reactor near the town of Dimona. The nuclear deterrent, while unable to cope with Arab hostility, was to change the rules of the strategic game by creating "a Middle East without war".[32]

The "Dimona syndrome" may be found in every page of a book published by Peres shortly after the signing ceremony in Washington. This is a fascinating document because it reveals the cultural presuppositions underlying the knowledge–power nexi which constructed the nuclear reactor, ventured to fight the populist trends of the 1980s, and engaged in stabilizing Israeli–Palestinian relations in the 1990s. In all these endeavours, professional knowledge was to provide a cure, or perhaps a diversion, from nationalist, populist and fundamentalist forces posing a danger – perceived in deterministic terms – to Israel.

In his book, Peres stresses the challenge of fundamentalism which, in his view, has been making deep inroads into the Middle East, endangering regional peace as well as individual government stability. Like populism in the 1980s, the fundamentalism of the 1990s poses a threat to the world cherished by the technocratic stratum, one marked by scientific progress, higher education, artificial intelligence and high technology. The answer to the fundamentalist challenge lies in a "systematized regional structure that will introduce a new framework for the region and that will provide the potential for economic and social growth, extinguishing the fire of religious extremism and cooling the hot winds of revolution".[33]

In venturing to extinguish fires and to cool hot winds, Peres yet again hinges upon professionalism, calling to amass its resources in order to overcome irrational obstacles: "Improvization will get us nowhere. Our plan must be professional, well reasoned, and well formulated, so that it can steer us in the right direction, turning theory into productive policy."[34] He aspires to nothing less than reshaping the entire Middle East and reconstructing its ideological climate. No wonder that he recalls his Dimona experience at the very beginning of the book. Like Dimona, his vision of peace reflects despair over the possibility of solving the problem of Israel's acceptance in the region without a total change in the rules of the game. It is also scarcely surprising that the book uses complex terminology as a way to overcome hard problems. Rather than viewing the Middle East in terms of nationalities being at each other's throat, Peres conceptualizes it as "a heterogeneous conglomeration of socioeconomic levels, standards of living, and per capita income".[35] Such a conglomeration can more easily be fixed with regional security systems, water projects, transportation and communication infrastructures and tourism industries.

Peres's vision of the new regional order includes a three-tiered pyramidal programme of cooperation, resembling the European project in the post-Second World War era. The first stage consists of binational or multinational projects, such as a joint research institute for desert management, or cooperative desalination plants. The second stage involves international consortiums carrying out projects which require large capital investments, such as a Red Sea–Dead Sea canal with free trade and tourism along its length, a joint Israeli–Jordanian–Saudi port, development of hydro-electric power for electricity and desalination, and well-planned, rapid development of Red Sea industries. The third stage includes regional community policies accompanied by the gradual development of official institutions.

The elaborate plan spelled out in the book reveals two main features which cross-cut the many projects: the precedence of economics over politics, and the formation of partnerships which can be instituted before borders are drawn and peace treaties signed. Peres attempts to construct a new reality in the Middle East in which business precedes politics and hence allows cooperation between peoples set apart by political differences.

Significantly enough, neither of these two central features has received due attention in the discourse over the Declaration of Principles. Commentators have stressed the DOP's political clauses: Israeli military withdrawal from Gaza and Jericho, the establishment of a Palestinian police force, elections to a Palestinian council which would assume responsibility for Palestinian self-rule and so on. These dimensions have particularly been stressed by the Palestinians to whom the assertion of power in Gaza and Jericho meant the beginning of Palestinian sovereignty. However, the declaration does not mention sovereignty, nor does it provide answers to the question of borders, refugees, the fate of Jewish settlements, or the question of Jerusalem, all of which are postponed to a later stage in the negotiations.

At the same time, the DOP includes a long list of projects along the lines elaborated in Peres's book. It includes an agreement to establish an Israeli–Palestinian continuing committee for economic cooperation, and focuses, *inter alia*, on cooperation in the fields of water, electricity, energy, finance, transport and communications, trade, industry, labour relations, human resources development, environmental protection, communication and media. In all these fields, development programmes are called for, to be prepared by experts on both sides.

In addition, the DOP includes a protocol on Israeli–Palestinian cooperation concerning regional development programmes initiated by the G-7 in cooperation with other states, including regional Arab states and institutions, as well as members of the private sector. The development programme, it says, will consist of an economic development programme for the West Bank and Gaza, including a social rehabilitation and housing programme, a small and medium business development plan, an infrastructure development programme and a human resources plan. It will also comprise a regional development programme, providing for the establishment of a Middle East development fund as a first step, and a Middle East bank as a second step; also included are the development of a joint Israeli–Palestinian–Jordanian plan for coordinated exploitation of the Dead Sea area, a canal from Gaza to the Dead Sea, a regional plan for agricultural development, interconnection of electricity grids, a regional tourism, transportation and telecommunications development plan and projects in other spheres.

In light of the many opportunities opening up here, it is hardly surprising that technocrats were the first to recover from the surprise caused by the Oslo Accords. As early as 1 September, Dani Gelerman, president of the commerce association, declared that the true test of the freshly-announced accords was the economic test: "If we prove that the quality of life in the territories increases, and Gaza indeed turns into an economic entity, we have made it."[36] On the same day, the economics editor of the popular daily *Yediot Acharonot* suggested that cooperation between Israelis and Palestinians ought to be based "not only on statesmen's understandings and bureaucrats' documents but, first and foremost, on direct contacts between Palestinian and Israeli entrepreneurs, investors, merchants, bankers and contractors". That editor, who in following weeks would become rather functional in legitimizing the Oslo Accords, promised his readers an "unprecedented economic boom".[37]

There were initial indications that a boom was in the coming. As intellectuals continued to debate the cognitive meaning of peace, the stock exchange rose dramatically, a process nurtured by declarations by managers in the public and private sectors on the blessings entailed by the DOP. Industrialists signed petitions linking peace with prosperity. Dan Proper, president of the industrialists' association gave an interview in which he foresaw "a glorious economic future" once a Middle East economic entity was formed, with 200 million consumers who could be expected to look to Israel as the natural financial centre.[38]

Thirty economists, members of a committee on economic issues related to Palestinian autonomy, submitted an optimistic report to the Minister of Finance, advocating a free flow of goods and services between Israel and the future Palestinian entity. Yet another committee recommended subsequent steps to be taken in the fields of commerce, labour relations, and fiscal and monetary policies. The warnings by one commentator that the Palestinians might take symbols of sovereignty more seriously than economic considerations passed virtually unnoticed.[39]

While the Declaration of Principles does involve "statesmen's understandings and bureaucrats' documents", it is largely an accord corresponding to the cultural predispositions and economic interests of Israel's technocratic stratum. It reflects the technocrat's predilection for combining political caution with technological fantasy. On the one hand, it avoids all political issues involving risks, and confines Palestinian self-rule to such limited spheres as education and culture, health, welfare, direct taxation and tourism. So much so that Palestinian intellectuals, not sharing the technocratic culture underlying the DOP, considered it a document of national surrender.[40] On the other hand, it proposes far-reaching projects of economic and technical cooperation, ignoring the fact that these projects are intended to be implemented by people engaged in a hundred-year war, in a region known for its fundamentalist moods, tribalist practices (such as blood vengeance) and nationalist sentiments.

The escapism involved cannot be overlooked. By ascending to the heights of technological vision, it is all too easy to evade the political hardships of a situation. The technocrat seems reluctant to deal with such matters as stones thrown by 12-year-old boys as part of the *intifada*. Questions regarding the essence of the conflict in the Middle East are postponed on the assumption that by the time they come to the negotiation table, a new reality will have emerged, based largely on technological development, which will demand different considerations.

Peres, for one, has put his faith for the future in the transformation of the Middle East from a system based on the nation-state to what he calls in his book "the Asiatic model of national politics, drawn from the world of economic values, whose fundamental principle is exploitation of knowledge in order to maximize profit".[41] He believes that on the threshold of the twenty-first century, professional knowledge has replaced nationalist, populist and fundamentalist sentiments as a leading force in the life of nations, and this might allow for the management of a Middle East marked by fundamental differences between people.

It is impossible to tell how much faith Peres really has in the capacity of technocrats to affect their overall environment. He must be aware that economic and technological cooperation is a slow process, severely challenged by fundamentalists who may not refrain from using the fruits of technology, such as modern means of propaganda and terrorism, to advance their cause. Always combining his technocratic inclinations with the patience of the cautious politician, Peres does not expect technological projects to revolutionize the Middle East to the extent of eliminating all rivalries. But he seems to believe that the global process in Europe and Asia – in which business interests help overcome historical hatreds, technical means of transportation and communication blur national boundaries, and regional development projects are conducted by political rivals – does not have to bypass Israel and its neighbours.

In this sense, Peres's change of partners for peace from King Hussein of Jordan in the 1980s to PLO Chairman Yasir Arafat in the 1990s has not been dramatic. In both cases he sought contact with forces in the Arab world which, he believed, had developed a strong enough technocratic stratum to have a stake in peace. This is where his pragmatism came to bear: for two decades Peres had been sponsoring secret negotiations with Jordanians, and later with Palestinians, who clearly did not represent the overall sentiment of their people towards Israel, but rather the businessman's and professional's interests. And in both cases, he was willing to strike a deal once he was convinced that the strata holding these interests had gained sufficient political viability to lead the road to cooperation with Israel.

Whether the technocrats on both sides of the Israeli–Palestinian divide can live up to this expectation and sustain the peace process is, perhaps, the hardest question of all. It could only be answered within a broad historical perspective. What can be stated at this point is that the

DOP, and possibly the peace process as a whole, bears all the hallmarks of that stratum, as demonstrated even in the speeches held in the signing ceremony in Washington. All speakers on the White House lawn used high language to mark the event: President Clinton spoke of peace of the brave, Secretary of State Warren Christopher of a dramatic step towards a just and comprehensive peace; Prime Minister Yitzhak Rabin mentioned love, dignity and freedom, while PLO Chairman Yasir Arafat spoke of peace, coexistence and equal rights.

But the speeches by the two functionaries who negotiated the DOP, Mahmoud Abbas of the PLO's Executive Committee and Israel's Foreign Minister Peres, differed in their technocratic language. Abbas mentioned peace not as a goal by itself but as "the only means to security and stability", linking it with cooperation, and stressing that economic development was the principle challenge facing the Palestinians. The main concern he conveyed was with "the struggle for growth and development which begins today". Peres's speech reflected a similar attitude. He, too, linked peace with cooperation, promised the Palestinians that "we mean business", called for the turning of "bullets to ballots", and claimed that the accord was underpinned by an economic structure as a way to achieve "political triumph and economic prosperity". "Let us become a civic community", he declared, calling for a region without wars in which "today's food is produced and tomorrow's prosperity is guaranteed, a region with a common market, a Near East with a long-range agenda".[42]

CONCLUSIONS

Israel's technocratic stratum, engaged in devising peace with the Arab world, has come under heavy attack by political fundamentalists who consider these efforts null and futile. To them, the right path lies in recognizing the tribal rules by which the Middle East has been operating for centuries. Some West Bank settlers, for instance, feel that Israel must resume the ancient biblical battles over settlement of the land, to be won by a combination of religious faith and military might. More moderate right-wingers aspire to reconciliation between Palestinians and Jews which would include acceptance of Israeli presence in the entire historic Land of Israel. Such reconciliation, they argue, would not come as a result of political and diplomatic accords but depends on the culmination of long historical processes.[43]

Some intellectuals on the left are using very similar language. Meron Benvenisti, for example, claims that the fundamental sources of the Arab–Israeli conflict could not be ignored. To him, a tribal–national–religious war between two communities that cannot be mustered through pragmatic arrangements is taking place. "A hundred-year war is not being solved by a *deus ex machina* landed in surprise", he wrote.⁴⁴ Like his rivals on the right, Benvenisti put his faith not in political accords but in the gradual transformation of people's perceptions and cognitions.

However, while the quest for cognitive changes that would allow Israel to integrate in the region is understandable, it is hard to find any signs that such a change is possible, whether in the short term or over the long run. Even those intellectuals who considered the Declaration of Principles a major cognitive breakthrough have had second thoughts once terrorism by rejectionists on both sides began to show its hand. It is therefore crucial that the pragmatism characterizing the DOP takes hold, notwithstanding the measure of escapism it involves. Rather than fight over national symbols, historic promises and holy places, one must design development projects concerning water, electricity, communication, transportation and so on, as a means to inspire a widespread – pragmatic – interest in regional cooperation. Such a technocratic approach may not satisfy the quest for "peace" propounded by most intellectuals; but there would seem to be no viable alternative to pragmatism, which promises at least some hope in great despair.

NOTES

1. Meron Benvenisti, "The Oslo Seminar",*Ha'aretz*, 2 Sept.1993.
2. Gabi Sheffer, "And They Divided This Land", *Ha'aretz*, 10 Sept. 1993.
3. Avraham Tal, "Five Million Insulted People", *Ha'aretz*, 2 Sept. 1993.
4. Ze'ev Schiff, "The Strategic Surprise", *Ha'aretz*, 2 Sept. 1993.
5. Amos Oz, "To Clear the Minefield in the Heart", *Yediot Acharonot*, 5 Sept. 1993.
6. Shulamit Hareven, "Moving", *Yediot Acharonot*, 31 Aug. 1993; Yizhar Smilansky, "Two Dreams, Two Wills, Two Claims", *Yediot Acharonot*, 13 Sept. 1993.
7. Beni Katzover, "Not With Violence – With Force!", *Yediot Acharonot*, 1 Sept. 1993; Naomi Frankel, "The Principle Supercedes the Law", *Yediot Acharonot*, 7 Sept. 1993.
8. Aharon Amir, "A Nightmare", *Ma'ariv*, 14 Sept. 1993.
9. Nachum Barnea and Shimon Shiffer, "The Hands Are Peres's Hands, but the Voice is the Voice of Rabin", *Yediot Acharonot*, 3 Sept. 1993.
10. Azami Bashara, "Certainly Yes and No", *Politika*, No.51 (Nov. 1993), p.18.
11. See Matti Golan, *The Road to Peace: A Biography of Shimon Peres*, New York, Warner Books, 1989.
12. Amos Perlmutter, *Military and Politics in Israel*, London, Frank Cass, 1969.
13. For a different definition of the "technocratic stratum", namely, as a group seeking rule by experts, see Frank Fischer, *Technocracy and the Politics of Expertise*, Newbury Park, CA, Sage, 1990.
14. Shimon Peres, *David's Sling*, London, Weidenfeld & Nicolson, pp.297–8.
15. Ibid., p.298.
16. *State of Israel: From the Knesset*, Jerusalem, Government Press Office, 22 Oct. 1984.
17. "Populism", as used in this study, refers to the replacement of orderly political structures by direct contact between leaders and the led. See Ghita Ionescu and Ernest Gellner (eds.), *Populism: Its Meanings and National Characteristics*, London, Weidenfeld & Nicolson, 1969; Norman Pollack, *The Just Polity: Populism, Law and Human Welfare*, Urbana, IL, University of Illinois Press, 1987.
18. Eliot Freidson, *Professional Powers: A Study of the Institutionalization of Formal Knowledge*, Chicago, University of Chicago Press, 1986; Donald A. Schon, *The Reflective Practitioner:*

How Professionals Think in Action, New York, Basic Books, 1983; Rolf Torstendahl and Michael Burrage (eds.), *The Formation of Professions: Knowledge, State and Strategy*, London, Sage 1990.

19. Theodor Herzl, *The Jewish State*, London, H. Pordes, 1972.
20. See, for example, Amos Elon, *The Israelis: Founders and Sons*, Harmondsworth, Penguin, 1981; A.B. Yehoshua, *Bizchut Ha'normaliut (In Favour of Normalcy)*, Jerusalem, Schoken, 1980; Amnon Rubinstein, *Me-Herzl ad Gush Emunim U'vahazara (From Herzl to Gush Emunim and Back)*, Jerusalem, Schoken 1980.
21. Dan Horowitz and Moshe Lissak, *Trouble in Utopia: The Overburdened Polity of Israel*, Albany, NY, State University of New York Press, 1990.
22. See Michael Bruno, *Crisis, Stabilization and Economic Reform*, Oxford, Oxford University Press, 1993.
23. See Michael Keren, "Law, Security and Politics", *International Journal of the Sociology of Law*, Vol.21 (1993); Michael Keren, "Economists and Economic Policy Making in Israel", *Policy Science*, in press.
24. See Michael Keren, *The Pen and the Sword: Israeli Intellectuals and the Making of the Nation-State*, Boulder, Westview Press, 1989; Haward M. Sachar, *A History of Israel: From the Aftermath of the Yom Kippur War*, New York, Oxford University Press, 1987.
25. See, for example, Thomas Friedman, "Getting Mideast Momentum Going Again", *New York Times, 27 Oct. 1985*.
26. *See, for example, Menahem Milson, "How Not to Occupy the West Bank", Commentary*, April 1986, pp.15–22.
27. Dan Horowitz, "The Israeli Concept of National security and the Prospects of Peace in the Middle East", in Gabriel Sheffer (ed.), *Dynamics of a Conflict: A Re-examination of the Arab-Israeli Conflict*, Atlantic Highlands, NJ, Humanities Press, 1975.
28. Peres, *David's Sling*.
29. Shimon Peres, "Strategy for a Transition Period", *International Security*, Vol.2 (Winter 1978), pp.10–12.
30. See, for example, Aryeh Shalev, "West Bank and Gaza Strip Autonomy", in Nimrod Novik and Joyce Starr (eds.), *Challenges in the Middle East: Regional Dynamics and Western Security*, New York, Praeger, 1981, pp.77–90.
31. Avi Shlaim, "Prelude to the Accord: Likud, Labor, and the Palestinians," *Journal of Palestine Studies*, Vol.23, No.2 (Winter 1994), pp.5–19.
32. Shimon Peres, *The New Middle East*, New York, Henry Holt, 1993, p.4.
33. Ibid., p.62.
34. Ibid., p.72.
35. Ibid., p.74.
36. Interviewed in *Yediot Acharonot*, 1 Sept. 1993.
37. Sever Plotzker, "The Economic Aspect", *Yediot Acharonot*, 1 Sept. 1993.
38. Dan Proper, "Peace is an Excellent Business", *Yediot Acharonot*, 3 Sept. 1993.
39. Ephraim Rainer, "Palestinian Work First", *Ha'aretz*, 22 Sept. 1993.
40. Edward Said, "The Morning After", *London Review of Books*, 21 Oct. 1993, pp.3–5.
41. Peres, *The New Middle East*, p.156.
42. All quotations are taken from: Government of Israel, *Declaration of Principles on Interim-Self-Government Arrangements*, Jerusalem, Ministry of Foreign Affairs, Sept. 1993.
43. Yair Sheleg, "The News Means Elimination", *Ha'aretz*, 3 Sept. 1993.
44. Meron Benvenisti, "The Oslo Seminar".

Index

www.ingramcontent.com/pod-product-compliance
Ingram Content Group UK Ltd.
Pitfield, Milton Keynes, MK11 3LW, UK
UKHW020429010325
455677UK00029B/1077